Local Regeneration Handbook

'In the beginning, there was nothing, which exploded'
(Terry Pratchett, *Lords and Ladies*, Gollancz, 1992)

'And God said, "Let there be Light"'
(*The King James Bible*, Genesis 1:3)

At school I was taught we need a healthy balance between
the mental, the physical and the spiritual.

You will need a strong world view to support you in the
regeneration jungle.

Local Regeneration Handbook

Andrew Maliphant

Cartoons by Kipper Williams

Los Angeles | London | New Delhi
Singapore | Washington DC | Melbourne

Los Angeles | London | New Delhi
Singapore | Washington DC | Melbourne

SAGE Publications Ltd
1 Oliver's Yard
55 City Road
London EC1Y 1SP

SAGE Publications Inc.
2455 Teller Road
Thousand Oaks, California 91320

SAGE Publications India Pvt Ltd
B 1/I 1 Mohan Cooperative Industrial Area
Mathura Road
New Delhi 110 044

SAGE Publications Asia-Pacific Pte Ltd
3 Church Street
#10-04 Samsung Hub
Singapore 049483

Editor: Robert Rojek
Editorial assistants: John Nightingale and
    Catriona McMullen
Production editor: Katherine Haw
Copyeditor: Jane Fricker
Proofreader:Andy Baxter
Indexer: Andrew Maliphant
Marketing manager: Susheel Gokarakonda
Cover design: Stephanie Guyaz
Typeset by: C&M Digitals (P) Ltd, Chennai, India
Printed in the UK

Library of Congress Control Number: 2017938371

British Library Cataloguing in Publication data

A catalogue record for this book is available from the
British Library

ISBN 978-1-5264-2698-7
ISBN 978-1-5264-2699-4 (pbk)

At SAGE we take sustainability seriously. Most of our products are printed in the UK using FSC papers and boards.
When we print overseas we ensure sustainable papers are used as measured by the PREPS grading system.
We undertake an annual audit to monitor our sustainability.

'Andrew Maliphant has produced the first book on regeneration to be written from the perspective of the practitioner for other practitioners. Drawing upon extensive personal experience the book outlines the opportunities and pitfalls in the field, identifying the personal skills which are necessary to perform what is often a complex and demanding role. The settings and challenges may vary but all regeneration practitioners will recognise the authentic voice of a professional attempting to improve localities.'

Jon Talbot, Centre for Work Related Studies, University of Chester

'Andrew Maliphant makes the art of local regeneration easy and practical for student and practitioner in this exciting and user friendly handbook. No stone is left unturned in his comprehensive advice on the purpose of regeneration and the teamwork critical to it, the pitfalls to avoid and the thematic context. He debunks the myths surrounding the regeneration types in the sustainable development and planning contexts, with clarity, in layman's terms. His analysis of the operational aspects of regeneration (managerial and financial) is indispensable for all readers serious about involvement in local sustainability projects.'

Chris Borg, National Association of Local Councils

'For both the practitioner and the novice, this handbook is a brilliant guide into the world of regeneration. Providing an historic, academic and practical insight into a subject that can often confuse and overwhelm us. Case studies bring the concepts to life, making it relatable – and enabling the reader to identify the importance of a holistic approach as "regeneration" is presented in all its guises. The injection of humour and tips to navigate the jargon bring a smile to the reader, and genuinely make the book an educational delight.'

Alison Robinson, CEO of Gloucestershire Association of Parish & Town Councils

Contents

About the Author

Andrew Maliphant has been working in regeneration since 1988, when he left the private sector to study Heritage Management at the Ironbridge Institute in Shropshire – in effect the first UK postgraduate course in all aspects of regeneration.

Since then he has worked on town centre regeneration in Ulverston in Cumbria, in Cinderford in the Forest of Dean and in the City of Gloucester, and on breaking cycles of deprivation in Oxfordshire housing estates, all of which required partnership working across all sectors to deliver multi-agency projects. He is now working on local regeneration as a clerk for a rural parish in Gloucestershire, having been chair of a community library cooperative, and coordinator of a project to support new start-up businesses. He describes what he does as 'helping people to help themselves'. Andrew has published articles on sustaining community projects based on environmental work in Hampshire, and a perspective on the social regeneration of Gloucester city centre, but this is his first book.

About the Cartoonist

From a central London studio, Kipper Williams draws for newspapers, magazines, audio visual presentations and greetings cards. Clients include *The Guardian*, *The Sunday Times*, *The Spectator*, *Private Eye*, *Country Life*, *John Lewis Gazette*, *Recharge*, *Broadcast*, *Engineering and Technology*, *Radio Times*, *Coaching at Work*.

Kipper has provided drawings for a number of books, and his cartoons have been acquired by the British Museum, the Victoria and Albert Museum and the Cartoon Art Trust. His collection of cartoons *All in Tents and Porpoises – The Best of Kipper Williams* was published by Amberley in 2016.

Prologue

Regeneration is about change.

I am still learning about regeneration, of places and communities, but I would like to share what I think I have learnt from people and experience over the past 25 years. This is by way of a contribution to the next 25 years, when local sustainability and leadership will be even more important than any national government support.

I make no apology for writing from a people perspective. As both actors and beneficiaries in regeneration, people are key to improving their own world. People can find money, but money on its own can't find the right people to make the right changes happen.

This book is based on experience in the UK, and its publication is one response to the new conditions that have developed there in recent times. One common message for all readers, wherever they live, is that they question received wisdom from any quarter in the light of local conditions. We know broad sweeping statements or policies do not fit every situation, so be careful of change, and carry out due diligence.

Change can be a quicksand. This book aims to help you find your own way through.

I owe a huge debt to all the communities it has been my privilege to work alongside. I must thank all those whose insights have helped me over the years – theirs is not the blame for the finished result. In particular I would like to dedicate this book to Sue Millar, Heritage Management course tutor when I studied at the Ironbridge Institute 1988–89, who was passionate about making connections.

Thanks

I would like to thank all those who helped by reviewing early drafts of this book, including:

- Alison Robinson, Gloucestershire Association of Parish and Town Councils

- Ed Wallis, Locality

- Francis Gobey, Gloucestershire County Council

- Jessica Steele, Jericho Road Solutions

- John Seddon, Gloucestershire County Council

- Dr Jon Talbot, University of Chester
- Mark Boyce, City Centre Community Partnership, Gloucester
- Paul Maliphant, Mott Macdonald Ltd
- Rachel Billings, Groundwork Derby & Derbyshire
- Richard Owen, Gloucester Heritage Urban Regeneration Company
- Roger Wade, Environment Agency Wales
- Stephen Cox, Mott Macdonald Ltd

My brother Paul has been particularly helpful with information from the engineering end of regeneration to match my own community perspective, and in asking telling questions about blanks in the book as a whole – thanks, bro.

Acknowledgements

I would like to record my thanks to the following for their particular insights and/or permission to quote from their work, with many apologies to anyone I may have inadvertently missed:

- The Buckland Newton Community Property Trust for the photograph and information about their community land trust

- Campaign to Protect Rural England (CPRE) and Gloucestershire Rural Community Council for the approach to neighbourhood planning

- Charles Dickens for the quote from Mr Micawber

- Cirencester Town Council for their approach to local town planning

- ClearlySo for the Green Rooms investment story

- David Kolb for learning styles, and Peter Honey and Alan Mumford for further development of the concept

- The *Derry Journal* and *Londonderry Sentinel* for details of the life of Paddy Doherty

- The Derry Youth and Community Workshop for the photograph of Paddy Doherty outside the Heritage Library

- Douglas McGregor for the hierarchy of needs

- The Freedom Bakery for the photograph and information about their project

- Book of Genesis chapter 1 verse 3

- *The Guardian* originally published the cartoons in Chapters 4 and 7

- Helen Melia for her advice on community finance

- Helen Quigley for the future plans of the Inner City Trust, Londonderry

- Incredible Edible Todmorden for the photograph and information about their project and approach

- The Intergovernmental Panel on Climate Change for publishing data from several scientific surveys on CO_2 in the atmosphere

- Janis Stanford for her insights into negotiation

- The Joseph Rowntree Foundation for their definition of poverty

- Kipper Williams for the twelve great cartoons in the text
- Kristoffer Boesen for information on Scottish community councils
- Llanelli Rural Council for the photograph and information about their approach to the Wellbeing of Future Generations (Wales) Act
- Mark Durkan MP for his eulogy of Paddy Doherty
- Matt Lally for his steps to good masterplanning
- Miranda Jenkins for the questions for start-up businesses
- Neil Troughton for his advice on shared space
- The Orange Group Ltd for the types of leadership
- Percy Bysshe Shelley for 'Ozymandias'
- *Private Eye* for permission to reproduce the cartoon in Chapter 12
- Richard Partington for 'ethnic cleansing by money'
- Rob Hopkins in Totnes for the Transition movement
- Rudyard Kipling for 'Six Honest Serving Men'
- Sevenoaks Town Council for the photograph and details of the Stag Community Arts Centre project
- Society of Local Council Clerks (SLCC) for their magazine *The Clerk* in which details of parish council projects are published
- Staunton Parish Council for details of their parish plan SWOT analysis
- Sue Millar for the approach to project management
- Swansea Community Energy and Enterprise Scheme for the photograph and information about their project
- Terry Pratchett for the opening quotation taken from *Lords and Ladies* (Gollancz, 1992)
- The coiners of 'Mickey Marx Economics', whoever they were
- UK government for the definition of sustainable communities
- UNESCO (United Nations Educational, Scientific and Cultural Organization) for the definition of culture, and Andrew Fox for its suggested sub-division
- Wendy Davis from the Women's Design Service (now with Rooms Of Our Own) for her definition of the really hard-to-reach groups

All photographs are by the author unless otherwise stated.

Preface for Academe

This book is a departure from past texts looking at policies and case studies. It is aimed at giving an insight into how to deliver practical regeneration on the ground, while retaining standards of academic rigour – and still with some case studies to add colour to process, and provide exemplars for action.

> As regeneration is a human activity, some of the human references I have found to be part and parcel of local success will be included from my own and others' experience, but identified in boxed print like this to distinguish them from more formal regeneration processes.

I met a young postgraduate student in Manchester some years ago who was planning to turn his regeneration qualification into employment in regeneration, so whether as a perspective or a practical guide, I hope your students will find this text useful.

Preface for Local Regeneration

This book is written as if speaking to a single worker leading local regeneration – but it may be that you are from a group such as a parish council that hasn't yet appointed anyone to that task, be it the parish clerk or someone else.

In terms of finding the right person, there are of course skills like project management you can find from CVs, and local knowledge you can clarify at interview. But rather than plump for someone who may seem on the surface to be an obvious local candidate, may I suggest you look for someone who is:

- Inclusive – naturally good at bringing people together to achieve a shared result

- Outgoing – naturally goes out to find solutions to any issue that comes up, with the determination to see them through

- Multi-tasking – capable of keeping several balls in the air at once

- Self-aware – knows when to bring in other pairs of hands rather than insist on doing it all themselves

- Modest – happy with a shared success rather than aiming for all the credit

The person to be wary of is loud, outspoken, and a leader in the sense of the Roman centurion ('I say to a man, Go, and he goeth') rather than someone with wider leadership and diplomacy skills who will bring together all the talents in a team without needlessly upsetting people. Because you will need everyone onside to be sure of success.

And if you are an individual just starting a local regeneration campaign – power to your elbow! Keep that conviction that things can be better.

Now read on …

Introduction

This book is about regenerating places where people live and work.

I say this at once to distinguish what I mean by regeneration from the many other meanings given to the word by various other professions, and that invariably crop up whenever I search 'regeneration' on the Internet!

Even having narrowed the definition so far, there is still a debate between people who come to regeneration with very differing perspectives and agendas, which I guess is healthy. My own definition of regeneration, rural as well as urban, is that it is change for the better – change that helps an area and its inhabitants to be better able to sustain themselves in future – and in broad terms this definition assumes that past solutions are no longer working and that another approach is needed.

There have been a number of academic textbooks about urban regeneration in particular, many focusing on government policy, and some collections of articles around best practice, but no practical handbook that says 'this is what you do'. My plan is to provide such a guide written in readable English, and I hope I have in some measure succeeded.

I have addressed this book to a character I have called a local regeneration worker. This could be anyone from a concerned and active member of the community to a public sector official to a special regeneration project officer. What I would say they should all have in common is a concern for the wellbeing of the community where they live or work, and an ability to work with others for the best possible future for that community.

I have taken this approach after some 25 years' personal experience in order to distinguish genuine people- and place-based regeneration from urban development. Development for private or corporate objectives may have some regenerative effect – it may even look like change for the better, and certainly will be described as such – but by its nature it won't be designed primarily for community benefit, and as a result it won't always have a lasting good effect on the community or the place that it says it serves.

It is much better I would say to focus on sustainable local benefit from the outset.

The Background to Regeneration

Just a bit of potted history before we get our sleeves rolled up.

Many of the key developments in what became known as the industrial revolution began in England, and the whole of the United Kingdom (England,

Scotland, Wales and Northern Ireland) rose to industrial might and world power which arguably reached its peak in the Victorian era at the end of the 19th century, when the USA and Germany were also challenging for the top spot. Technological successes were exported throughout the world, but since the end of the artificial boom created by the First World War, competition from other nations (partly helped by lower costs of living in those countries) has been a major factor in the progressive eclipse of the UK such that in the long term the wealth of the nation has slowly but steadily declined.

This is not to say that attempts have not been made to stem the tide. Apart from general government support and the encouragement of British manufacture and exports, a number of industrial and trading estates have been built in what were felt to be good locations, with some schemes to help people relocate from depressed areas to those of labour shortages, as well as major changes to cities in the 1960s and beyond. Many of these approaches were predicated on growth which didn't happen in the way expected, and some unfortunately tore apart existing urban fabric and communities.

In July 1981 riots erupted in Toxteth, a suburb of the major industrial city and port of Liverpool in northern England. These were followed by unrest throughout the country, much of it focused on the police, but leading to an increasing focus on the underlying causes of the riots, many of them seen as economic.

Led by Michael (now Lord) Heseltine, then a member of the British (UK) parliament and member of the Cabinet, the UK government developed a new series of schemes whereby government funds were injected into selected areas as the basis for improving local prospects. This policy extended across party political boundaries and arguably reached its peak under the New Labour government of Tony Blair which continued the 'Single Regeneration Budget' (SRB) schemes of the previous Conservative government. As many of the areas needing assistance were ex-industrial or otherwise neglected areas, this process became widely known as regeneration, and that process based on central government funding is what is commonly understood by regeneration in the UK to this day.

However, times have changed. The UK government no longer has funds to spend on regeneration in this way, and the coalition which came to power in 2010 ushered in a period of austerity which has cut local government funding by a third. This means that local government has no ring-fenced funding or statutory remit for regeneration either, and without statutory responsibility things may only get worse.

The need for local improvements will always be there, however, while national conditions and the value of top-down central management remain uncertain. A global financial crisis in 2008, caused originally by the overselling of mortgages in the USA and subsequent high level of defaulting but with other factors as well, spread throughout the international banking world. The UK government had to intervene to help stabilise the situation, including buying a large share in UK financial institutions, notably the Lloyds TSB banking group and the Royal Bank of Scotland. I noted in 2013:

- UK unemployment is over 7%, including over a million young people who see few prospects, with even higher unemployment in some urban areas

- Interest rates are at an all-time low, and the Governor of the Bank of England advises that interest rates will be kept low for at least another three years

- Accordingly, at least one of the major UK banks has difficulty recommending to its customers how to invest what money they have

- Food banks are springing up all over the country, and in all kinds of areas – and being used by professional people who have difficulty finding work

- Apart from applauding manufacturing/export successes, and funding searches for 'innovation' to try to regain a technological edge over the rest of the world, the UK government's main domestic solution seems to be encouraging house building on green countryside, to encourage some employment in the short term, and in response to the fact that new households are currently being formed more quickly than new houses being built (and not just through immigration)

- There has been recent newspaper speculation about how many people in the UK genuinely have funds to fall back on in case of need

Unemployment has since eased, but the government focus on new housing at all costs remains, with housing targets being effectively forced on local authorities. A Bank of England 'stress test' in late 2016 revealed that the still 73% government-owned Royal Bank of Scotland was the worst prepared for another financial crisis. And following the 2017 UK general election campaign we are being offered a range of political options for government to cover the costs of public services that are under increasing pressure from an ageing population.

I won't go on (and I won't talk about leaving the European Union either!) – other nations will have experienced similar conditions to these, and very much worse, but all this is relatively new to the UK and newly realised. This book looks at how local communities may still 'regenerate' their own local areas without the luxury of large government grants – or even, how they might do it better, with local rather than national direction.

The Benchmark – Sustainable Development

Would you call something regeneration if it failed the next year?

In difficult times there is a great temptation to leap on any suggestion for local improvements, especially if outside bodies are proposing to bring in money, but it's foolish to rush in before you're sure there will be a long-lasting and good result.

The best benchmark that has been identified so far is a question derived from the 1987 report of the World Commission on Environment and Development

(1987), *Our Common Future* (commonly called the Brundtland Report after the Commission's chairman Gro Harlem Brundtland): 'Can we meet the needs of the current generation without reducing the capability of future generations to meet their own needs?' In practical terms, long-lasting regeneration needs to be based on what has been called the three-legged stool of sustainable development:

- Physical sustainability – are we making the best use of local land and resources, will what we do make any future uses impossible?

- Social sustainability – will what we are doing bring the local community together, and will it encourage people to continue to work together in the future?

- Economic sustainability – perhaps the most difficult of all to gauge, will what we do bring jobs and prosperity both now and in the future?

The heart of this book lies in helping to make informed decisions about what is best for the future of your community, following these principles. A large claim, but we can but try.

The Framework for Local Regeneration

Part of the difficulty facing a local regeneration worker is the conflict between macro (national) and micro (local) views of the world. Twenty-five per cent of the wealth of the UK is generated by the City of London, which can have a disproportionate effect on the views of the UK government who are based nearby. It's hard for other areas of the UK to find a resonance with London-based national views when local needs are so much closer to home, and there is also less written material about these local concerns – and every area is different anyway, with different needs and opportunities.

There is plenty enough for a regeneration worker to do, from identifying local needs, to engaging local people and organisations in finding the solutions. Creating effective local partnerships and bringing in financing are only two of the common steps towards a successful result. There will also be people and players to deal with who are coming with very different agendas, and who *don't* have the wellbeing of the community at heart – denizens of what I call the regeneration jungle.

There is a 'trickle-down' philosophy to be wary of, a self-satisfying concept that bringing in outside investment and developing new buildings and ventures will automatically benefit the needy residents of the area in question. I attended a conference in Liverpool in 2004 and heard community workers from Toxteth complaining that despite millions spent in Liverpool since 1981 the people of Toxteth had found no significant improvement in their lot. Recent history in the UK – banks having to be bailed out by the government, stock market crashes – should make us wary of the idea that big money of itself is always the answer.

There is also the question of the changing environment – global warming, green energy, food costs and food supply. People are dealing with local change when the very rules of (peacetime) living on the Earth are under review, and when the supply of public sector funding is squeezed and uncertain, particularly in the UK. This double whammy requires a combination of sharp focus and open-mindedness from all those involved in leading regeneration.

I would say the crucible for a final definition or framework for regeneration lies in an area bounded by a number of conflicts:

- Local and national perspectives

- Individual and corporate agendas

- Political ambition and community need

A regeneration worker will need to marshal and somehow satisfy all these forces in order to make a difference (change) on the ground.

Let's focus on regeneration as change that helps the people and place in question to be better able to sustain themselves in future, without public subsidy, and harness public and private ambitions to that end.

So, now for the chase.

1
Why Regenerate?

Let's say you want the place where you live to both look better and operate more effectively for the benefit of its residents and its businesses.

Do you think you know all the local issues and all the answers for a better future for your area? Sometimes we do – but let's double-check the 'why' of what we're thinking about before we get bogged down in the detail of the 'what' and the 'how'.

We should look at local aspirations, local strengths, weaknesses, opportunities and threats (SWOT analysis), and collect solid evidence to back it all up, as potential funders will want to know that we've covered the detail.

Energetic activists may not want to go to this level of detail and prefer to rush straight ahead to plan their regeneration campaign – with maybe more action than planning. I suggest we should spend the time to make sure that what we do will be long-lasting before we spend resources badly, and even if we fast forward from Chapter 1 to Chapter 8, use the other chapters for reference.

The other major benefit of coming up with a clear 'why' – perhaps expressed in a few words as a 'mission statement' – is that it will help keep you focused. Once you start a regeneration campaign, and in particular once you start being successful, all kinds of people will come to you with suggestions for new projects. In order to keep focused on the best use of your time, a clear 'why' will help you identify which projects are for you, and which – short of a bit of publicity support – should be managed by somebody else.

What's It All About?

We know regeneration is a change process, but each place will have its own ideas about what to change into.

Research in Gloucester city centre in 2005 suggested that 50% of people equated regeneration with physical change – building new buildings, improving old buildings.

Another 25% felt the most important thing was to involve local people and businesses in decisions about the future – it was the *way* it was done which was key.

The rest of the survey replies were more detailed, very particular comments of different kinds, reflecting individual concerns.

Is this how it is in your area?

We need to find out what local people think is important, as whatever we do, we will be more successful if we carry the whole community with us.

Depending on the size of our community, a couple of open days (one in working hours, one not) at fully accessible venues where people can look at new and old photographs and ask questions is good, and any survey forms should also be made available electronically for busy or housebound computerate people.

Hard copy surveys can be expensive for a large community, but may be handy if you can get volunteers to deliver them as not everyone uses computers. We devised a simple street survey in the summer of 2011 when we were gathering ideas to inform a parish plan for Mitcheldean in the Forest of Dean. We just asked three questions:

- What do you like about Mitcheldean?

- What don't you like?

- What could be improved?

The feedback from this and from additional comments at a public event formed the basis for a detailed questionnaire that went round all local households and businesses, and the results formed the basis for the final plan.

Parish plan exhibition in Mitcheldean community centre August 2011

Local Identity

What is so special about the place considering regeneration?

- Its location?

- Its history and culture?

- Its raw material and industries?

I could say its people, but that goes without saying – and they need to be involved in these discussions anyway.

Don't pick a future that doesn't make sense locally – not everywhere can be a major shopping centre, for example. The city council in Birmingham based their regeneration plans on the city's handy location in the middle of England, with good transport routes, and it became the site for the National Indoor Arena. They also undid the isolation of the city centre caused by 1960s ring roads for the mighty motor car.

There is a 'Transition movement' view that every place should be replanning its future anyway, as so many past assumptions about things like financial markets, climate and the availability of resources now need to give way to greater local resilience. So the way forward may not be the mixture as before – though something that worked locally 50 or 150 years ago should be discussed rather than dismissed out of hand, as at least it worked once!

Get local people and organisations together, and carry out a SWOT analysis (list strengths, weaknesses, opportunities and threats) for the local area. Then put together statistical figures for the identified issues to create a 'baseline', so that you can measure progress over time. Success can then be judged on whether the measured figures are going up (e.g. employment) or down (e.g. crime) as appropriate.

Is there a regional context? Look at other similar places, spend some time on picking a direction, and then work at 'place making' together. Involving local people in determining local identity and what the future should look like is absolutely crucial. I firmly believe that most local issues, even if they seem to be subject to national policy, can only be really dealt with at a local level where the detail is known, rather than having solutions imposed on a community from above.

SWOT Analysis

This is a well-established process for setting the parameters for your local regeneration scheme, for example:

- Strengths – such as the value of your location for business, skills levels of local people, local amenities such as sporting facilities, strong local heritage

- Weaknesses – declining industries, high levels of unemployment and crime, low levels of health and wealth

- Opportunities – sites available for redevelopment or a new local market, government grant schemes, developer interest

- Threats – environmental issues like rising flood levels

Some issues you may find cropping up under more than one heading, such as a good road network providing economic opportunities but environmental threats. This is fine – a bit of perspective helps produce a balanced plan for the way ahead. And a clear SWOT analysis can help if you are ever faced with the dilemma of trading off one aspect of sustainability against another.

Evidence Base

You will need to find some clear facts and measures to fill out your SWOT analysis, such as:

- Local population – numbers, ages, genders, ethnicity, health and lifestyle issues
- Local businesses – types, numbers employed
- Local employment levels, including those who commute to work
- Local landowners (particularly of sites that need a new future)

Much of this detail can be found either through the Internet or by taking advice from local government sources.

We know quite a lot about regeneration now, and have access to local, regional, national and international statistics and UK good practice, for example:

- *Learning the Lessons from the Estates Renewal Challenge Fund* (Pawson et al., 2005)
- *The Single Regeneration Budget: Final Evaluation* (Rhodes et al., 2007)
- *Final Report on the New Deal for Communities Programme* (Batty et al., 2010)

Such reports along with properly charted local views, resources and aspirations will give us a much more solid basis for going forward.

> The angel is in the detail.
>
> Actually, there's only one job in regeneration, which is effectively marshalling all the detail and then applying it in the right place and in the right way with the right people.
>
> You heard it first here.

Outputs and Outcomes

What exactly are you trying to achieve? Measurable targets are very necessary to help focus a regeneration programme, but adopt them carefully, they're better as a skeleton than a straitjacket:

- **Mission statement** – a one-phrase summary of what you're trying to achieve, such as 'Reduce local crime and the fear of crime'

- **Outputs** – things you can number, such as new community safety publications, and new closed-circuit television (CCTV) cameras in place

- **Outcomes** – the result of your activities, such as less fear of crime measured through public surveys

- **Indirect outcomes** – things that happen as a side-effect of your activity, such as reduced insurance premiums in previously high-crime areas

- **Performance indicators** – measures that show progress towards a particular objective, such as reductions in the number of burglaries over time

- **Milestones** – can seem like outputs, but are really stage markers in a project or process, such as local shops signing up to participation in a crime reduction campaign

In the UK a number of measures have been grouped into the 'English Indices of Deprivation' which are re-measured every three years (see Appendix 1). Bringing areas out of 'deprivation' (horrible word) is therefore a common regeneration target, though finding some generic positive measures would be good, and some of us are working on that.

Before UK government funding was cut, there was what I call a 'percentage rugby' (concentrating on the parts of the game likely to produce the best result) approach to regeneration in the UK, focusing on the 70% of issues around finance, skills qualifications, jobs and new buildings. A lot of UK regeneration funding has been predicated on economic outputs such as new jobs, training courses and workspaces, but this reflects a received view that these are the most important things – which are happily measurable!

There are other things as important to community life, some of them spiritual, and not everyone in the community will put 'jobs' at the top of their list anyway (don't assume – ask them). So take any public funding by all means, but balance the official outputs with more local outcomes. Let's not marginalise what the community want for themselves – people do not live by bread alone – and let's go for the whole lot. If we don't, I strongly suggest we're admitting a degree of failure even before we start.

Poverty

> Jesus said 'The poor are always with you'. He never thought this would be underwritten by the UK government, who have since defined poverty in the UK as any family earning less than 60% of mean national income. So there'll always be someone in the UK who's officially poor.

The Joseph Rowntree Foundation's definition of poverty is 'when a person's resources are not enough to meet their basic needs'. This UK-based charity and research organisation has expanded on this statement to say:

> Poverty means not being able to heat your home, pay your rent, or buy the essentials for your children. It means waking up every day facing insecurity, uncertainty, and impossible decisions about money. It means facing marginalisation – and even discrimination – because of your financial circumstances. The constant stress it causes can overwhelm people, affecting them emotionally and depriving them of the chance to play a full part in society.
>
> The reality is, almost anyone can experience poverty. Unexpected events such as bereavement, illness, redundancy or relationship breakdown are sometimes all it can take to push us into circumstances that then become difficult to escape.

(Joseph Rowntree Foundation, 2016: 4)

The Foundation has carried out four years of research and in 2016 produced a strategy entitled *We Can Solve Poverty in the UK* (see Bibliography). In summary:

> Our five-point plan to solve poverty in the UK will:
> - Boost incomes and reduce costs;
> - Deliver an effective benefit system;
> - Improve education standards and raise skills;
> - Strengthen families and communities; and
> - Promote long-term economic growth benefiting everyone.

Bringing together the skills and resources of national and local governments, businesses, service providers and citizens, we want to solve poverty in the UK within a generation. Our vision is to make the UK fit for the children starting school this year – so that by the time they enter adulthood in 2030, they will be living in a UK where:

- No one is ever destitute;

- Less than one in ten of the population are in poverty at any one time; and

- Nobody is in poverty for more than two years.

(Joseph Rowntree Foundation, 2016: 5)

We can see from this that the Foundation also expect poverty to be a permanent local feature, but are proposing permanent ways to address it. These include actions that can be addressed locally:

- Improving people's skills and education

- Getting them into work that pays

- Reducing prices for essential goods and services (including housing)

- Unlocking the full human capital available

Many of the recommendations in the report focus on government-level action around support and social benefits, but the strategy also says, 'Galvanise community-led approaches and social action to build pressure for change'. I won't steal all the report's thunder here, but as we are clear there are poverty issues everywhere, then addressing poverty has to be one of the big concerns of a regeneration worker.

On the same topic, child poverty has been described as young people growing up in poor households. I mention child poverty because it's an inflammatory phrase, and can focus public attention on short-term relief for poorer children rather than the longer-term issue of what they and their families need to help get sustainable (probably work-based) income that will help lift them out of poverty forever. Child poverty is adult poverty too.

I make this point not to object to help for poor children, which of course is important, but as another word of warning before we rush into the 'what' and 'how'. You may have an idea of what you want to achieve in regeneration, but take time to check out the long-term impacts of what you're doing, don't just leap into the first idea that occurs that seems to make sense. Lasting long-term regeneration is the real prize.

Cycles of Deprivation

Some of the regeneration issues you may be trying to address will have been embedded for a long time, particularly in large housing estates in ex-industrial areas where three generations of the same family may be out of work. Such situations have been somewhat unhappily dubbed 'cycles of deprivation', though there are probably several cycles that need to be understood together:

- **Individual** – e.g. personal disappointment leading to lack of enthusiasm, leading in turn to indifferent response to new opportunities, thus increasing the chances of further disappointment; also the risk of poorer health through depression and lack of activity

- **Generational** – i.e. poor conditions in parents' lives that increase the risk of poor outcomes for their children

- **Neighbourhood** – i.e. wider sociological, economic and physical factors linked to the location

We carried out some work on this in Oxfordshire in 2010, looking at areas like Blackbird Leys, which is still suffering from the closure of the nearby Cowley motor works in the 1970s. Change in such areas will not come quickly, but we came to the following conclusions drawn from the evidence of past schemes and studies:

- 'Business as usual' is not sufficient to break deprivation

- Public services can and do improve prospects for individual families, but for the overall 'deprivation scores' of an area to change, it must also become a place where people want to work and live

- A real prospect of a better life helps people to want to develop their futures in an area

- In areas of high 'deprivation', this almost certainly means one or more radical changes to the area and to its long-term opportunities, including links to the wider economy

- All the evidence suggests that including local people in determining and delivering these changes is vital for their success

- Focusing all local agencies' efforts is also vital

- The process will take more than the five or ten years of previous schemes

At the risk of leaping ahead, this was our proposed template for breaking cycles of deprivation, which you might want to compare to the picture in your own area:

A place to work

- A variety of real opportunities for sustainable employment, greater than the number of local people needing work, and either provided locally or through travel to work

- Clear career routes to this employment, including information from employers about vacancies, access to the necessary foundation and vocational skills training, and planning and other policies to ensure local residents are given suitable priority

- Good access to adequate services to address any barriers to employment, including health services, childcare and debt counselling

A place to live

- Good quality mixed housing, affordable for all income levels, and set in a well-managed environment

- Good access to amenities, including shops, health centres and leisure facilities

- Good community cohesion and community safety, including vibrant community activities and local governance, with low levels of crime and anti-social behaviour

World View

I said at the start of this book that you will need a strong world view to support you in the regeneration jungle.

We'll hear more about the jungle later, but when dealing with a lot of complex issues with a large number of people, you can imagine that you will be glad of some touchstone or certainty of your own that you go back to when times get tough.

You may already have such a touchstone, but whether or not you do, try these three questions about the world you are seeking to change:

- How does it work?

- Who's really in charge of which bit?

- What matters for the future?

Having answers to these questions will help you to work out how to get to where you want to be. But remember, others on the same journey may have different answers to these questions, so check their world views also as you meet them along the way.

And do keep your own world view under review as you go. More information will inevitably become available.

Case Study: Staunton Parish Plan – SWOT Analysis

This is an example of a SWOT analysis carried out by local people when developing the 2007–2010 parish plan for Staunton in the Forest of Dean, Gloucestershire. An initial meeting was held in May 2006 with the support of the parish council to gauge the interest of residents in developing a plan.

The meeting included a SWOT analysis, and a steering group was subsequently formed.

It is interesting to see tourism identified as a threat as well as an opportunity – a common view in many attractive rural places – also they seem to have used STOW not SWOT. The definition given in the extract below explains the approach, though many of the opportunities are strictly speaking project ideas and community desires rather than, for example, the genuine tourism opportunities provided by the area for walkers and cyclists.

Strengths, Weaknesses, Opportunities, Threats

Strengths are the things which we are good at or are unique to our parish, such as an active community willing to help itself. We use our Strengths to overcome Weaknesses.

Opportunities are the things which either present themselves or are instigated by us to improve parish life. Threats are things which we may face now or those that a changing society presents such as burglaries or vandalism.

The following table was developed at our public meeting from parishioners and is recorded in order to capture those hopes and fears expressed there. It will serve as a guide to help us exploit our strengths and opportunities and better equip us to deal with weaknesses and threats.

Table 1.1 Staunton Parish Plan SWOT analysis

Strengths	Threats
The forest	Speed of traffic on A4136
Wild animals	Amount of heavy traffic on A4136
The scenery – beautiful landscape and good location	No crossing to link village across A4136
Quiet village life	Stowfield Quarry – the size – its expansion, the noise and pollution – worries about the explosions – worries regarding village houses
The village hall	
The Meend	Crime and vandalism
Active parish council for small parish	Rubbish
Local footpaths	Overgrown footpaths
Small population	Ageing population
Play area for children	Increasing house prices
Local community groups and clubs	Wild boar
Parish history	Apathy
Community spirit	Knotweed
Village pub	Dilapidated road surfaces
Active social groups	Closure of Church
Pleasant place to live	Sewerage
History	Tourism (also an opportunity)

(Continued)

(Continued)

Opportunities	Weaknesses
More clubs/activities	Division of village by road
Restore the Meend and stone walls	Lack of public transport
Tourism (also a threat)	Poor police street/Meend cover
Development of B&Bs	Limited facilities for young/elderly
Walking, cycling	Lack of local employment
Horse riding	Traffic speed and noise
Locally produced goods – village market	Inadequate car parking facilities
Plant more flowers	Poor communication especially for those new to village
Better signage	
Maps available for disabled and able bodied	New householders not participating in village community life
Pelican crossing	
Construction of village hall car park	

Source: Staunton Parish Council (2007: 15–16)

Further Reading

Burwood, Simon and Roberts, Peter (2002) *Learning From Experience*. BURA (British Urban Regeneration Association, now sadly no more) – the first publication I think that attempted to collate good regeneration practice in the UK – for example, 'The most successful schemes are those that address a range of issues by utilising a multi-dimensional approach to regeneration'. As a regeneration worker you will develop a matrix in your head of how modern life is managed, and by which agencies, to match against whatever issue comes up.

Independent Commission on Health Equalities in Oxfordshire (2016) *Headline Report: Addressing Health Inequalities in Oxfordshire*. National Health Service – one of a number of initiatives you can read up on, this one further developing the thinking in Oxfordshire around the impact of poverty – downloadable from http://healthwatchoxfordshire.co.uk/sites/default/files/health_inequalities_head line_report.pdf (Accessed 14 June 2017).

2
Team Work

If you've dived headlong into the first chapter, even if you've managed to collate what you think are all the necessary data, you've probably come out realising that regeneration is not a one-person project.

Good. Otherwise, hospital and failure beckon!

Whatever is best for the future of your area will require a lot of local people and companies and public organisations working together, and the first skill for a regeneration worker to cultivate is the ability to bring people together into a team.

(And if it's beyond you personally, find the local person who can do it with you.)

The Jungle

Team work is needed to get through the regeneration jungle alive – even inveterate and energetic explorers need help to deal with difficult people who have different agendas and use a different language (and who may not be shy about using weapons).

An early review of this book stated:

> All regeneration is local because that is where it takes place. However, in aggregate regeneration is a huge industry involving billions of pounds of investment. It is shaped by equally powerful forces set in train by long term economic and demographic change. Internationally it is also about geo-political and geo-economic shifts which involve a fight for survival for those nations on the wrong side of the curve. It involves competitive global marketing of countries, regions, cities and localities for highly mobile and now increasing scarce investment. That international capital also brings international corporations like Westfields to White City and Stratford with increasingly homogenous solutions.

> The players involved are frequently pension funds, absentee landowners who wish to extract maximum returns, developers who do not respect the planning process, consultants who do their clients' bidding, proposals which coat their over-development in a sugar coating, spurious consultation processes, local authority officers who are out of their depth and out gunned by their private sector adversaries and local communities that are under-resourced and at their wit's end.

This is not simply an urban issue, small towns and villages up and down the country are being held hostage by developers who have bought options on farm land on the edge of their communities and are seeking to transform them out of recognition.

So, regeneration won't be a cakewalk. As well as pursuing your own agendas, you will probably need the help of a team to deal with all these development threats, and to anticipate them wherever possible.

The 18th-century Russian General Suvorov coined the phrase 'Train hard, fight easy' – or as Lord Baden-Powell would put it, let's be prepared.

Tarzan

Just don't go there. Regeneration is not a solo effort, nor a star vehicle.

Partnership Working

Much maligned.

Has been compared to a marriage, but not in serious detail because guess what? Every marriage is different.

Partnership working is not about making things easier, it's about more work for a better quality result, because no matter what goodies everyone brings to the table, you still have to make the effort to work together, like it or not. Don't dump all the risk on one partner, for example, it doesn't inspire trust – and trust is the bedrock of partnership.

Who are the potential partners? These can include:

- Local government bodies – possibly councils at two or three different levels – both officers and elected councillors

- Local resident associations

- Local business associations

- Local landowners

- Local charities and voluntary associations

- Special interest groups focusing on topics such as local history and the environment

Many of these may not have dealt with each other before, or even been at odds with each other before, so bringing them together may not always be straight-forward, but you will need to be straight with them yourself so there is a common platform from the beginning. So – just like a marriage? – go into partnership working with your eyes open, and be prepared to be honest with your partners over everything so there is the best chance of agreement on a collective approach. And if it stops working – or clearly isn't going to work from the outset with one or more of the potential partners – then be clear but nice about not doing it, because who knows when you might need partner support again.

You almost certainly will need to get into a partnership with others to achieve regeneration, as there are so many aspects to modern life, with different agencies and people involved. The greater the partnership of course, the more the need for clear ground rules (possibly even a legal constitution), and clarity about the role for each partner, including who is in the chair. Also power will be spread unevenly, so stay alert.

As the local regeneration worker, you may then find yourself reporting progress and asking for decisions from a group of partners or a formal board. This requires a little discipline in circulating papers before meetings, while being aware of the differing views within the group and presenting your case accordingly. You will value the support of an even-handed chair, so try and influence the appointment of the right person. If you need one, try to find a friendly fixer in your area, and get their advice, but don't make any assumptions about people's motives, find out through one-to-one conversations.

Of course, regeneration partnerships should always include the local community, who can become upset if other partners are at war with each other. I always felt I was a guest in the places I was a regeneration worker, and there was a feeling of reporting to everyone, and that helped me to keep things in perspective.

Dark Arts

Managing your steering group is a dark art, particularly if they are the people paying you! Second only in darkness to the art of allowing someone to talk themselves out of something you know they really shouldn't be thinking of doing, such as writing a letter to the media that you know will come back to haunt them …

I honestly can't give you all the secrets here, but a number of readers will be nodding agreement already. You need to know everyone's interests, their skills, their sticking points and their pet projects. You need to notice the language they use, the company they keep, and their general outlook on life.

(Continued)

(Continued)

A simple example is this – you want to get your steering group to agree to something, but (partly because of representing different organisations and sectors) a single presentation to all of them probably won't work, because they all see things differently. Go round them individually, get their agreement based on their own perspectives, and when you're sure they're all onside, present your proposal simply at a meeting, perhaps as part of a wider scheme so it doesn't stick out. There's a bonus here in goodwill, as the group, who will know of their diverse backgrounds, will feel good that they have agreed something collectively, and the meeting will (hopefully) end in smiles.

And if you can't find agreement in advance, think again about your proposal ...

Joined-up Regeneration

You might think that bringing together physical, social and economic regeneration to satisfy the needs of sustainable development, as well as satisfying all local needs, is so obvious that everyone will be doing it.

You'd be wrong.

Most people are only comfortable with what they know, and are reluctant to interfere in what other people know well – making connections in real life and then doing something about it is unusual behaviour. Egging people on to do better in their own areas of expertise is even more unusual.

Even though we all know good housing and health and a job and access to services and opportunities for enjoyment and companionship are all part of making a person happy, putting together a regeneration programme to achieve all that and more is not common (though may it become so).

And though we know there are jobs in housing and health and services, and healthy people work better, and happier people are more likely to be healthy, we don't necessarily see that an integrated programme to address all these issues might deliver all the benefits more promptly and more sustainably than a few people focusing on one or two aspects only ('silo mentality') and leaving the rest to chance.

Sorry, preaching again. World view, anyone?

The crude 'virtuous circle' (as opposed to a vicious circle of decline) shown in Figure 2.1 is not a perfect illustration as it's an 'open system' not a 'closed system' – in other words, there's movement in and out of the circle that isn't shown. Negative factors such as economic or natural disasters will intrude, and so there will need to be other positive factors such as counselling and financial help to compensate.

Dealing with such a range of factors is a major argument for joined-up regeneration, as several agencies as well as the local community will need to be involved.

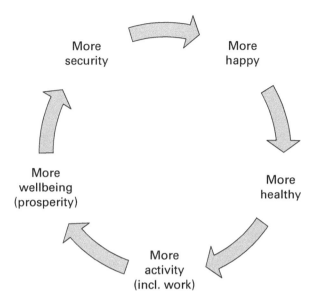

Figure 2.1 Virtuous circle

Also, the illustration as shown is about individuals – looking at it in community terms will bring another set of factors into play, though there is already one strong connection in that being part of a community is a prerequisite of 'activity' and 'wellbeing'.

I've deliberately talked about 'wellbeing' not just financial prosperity, just as 'activity' can be more than paid work. A job is very important but not enough to make everyone happy, there can be other fulfilling activity – and full employment is desirable but never straightforward, a lot of conditions need to be in place.

What I have called the 'percentage rugby' approach to regeneration tends to focus on getting people into work as the most obvious way to achieve prosperity, happiness and health. This is actually another good argument for joined-up regeneration, as several organisations will need to be involved to achieve this (see Training for Employment in Chapter 6), particularly in so-called deprived areas with high unemployment.

There are many other connections in life that mean disparate agencies have to work together, for example:

- Environmental health officers, local shops and tourism concerns working together on a programme for public toilets in a city centre

- Health trusts, sports development and parks officers working together to provide 'health walks'

(Continued)

(Continued)

- Police, developers and planners working together to build community safety into new housing and shopping areas ('Secured by Design' initiative)

These are simply examples from my own experience, and I cannot claim I saw any of them coming in advance. We should all keep an open mind about who needs to connect with whom in order to achieve effective regeneration.

So. If you want to help improve all aspects of people's lives, and are convinced about the benefits of joined-up regeneration, how do you persuade other people and agencies to join in?

Use a little psychology perhaps, for example:

- Natural joined-up thinkers are easy to talk to – naturally, they're interested in whatever you have to say – but they're probably doing too much themselves, so you'll need to keep in regular contact in order to work together.

- Those who only wish to do specific things in the way they understand may nevertheless be honest types – think about some joint training experiences with their peers that might influence their thinking. Short of getting round them via their bosses (difficult if they themselves are senior in their organisations), you may just have to be grateful that they do what they do.

- Single-topic experts who show interest in how their work affects economy, environment and society – this is a great opportunity, but be careful. Not everyone takes on ideas in the same way (see Learning in Chapter 9), so spend some good time with such people on developing their individual paths to joined-up working. Mass suggestion or preaching may not sustain matters, particularly when you're not in the room!

You are unlikely to get total cooperation – but that isn't the point, is it? Regeneration is not a one-person business. Try creating an informal group of people who between them cover a whole range of skills and expertise and interests, with a shared interest in regenerating your local area, apply what you know about helping people to work together and enjoy themselves, and see how you go.

For a city of 120,000 population, responding to a declared objective around the wider benefits of regeneration, I developed a circulation list of 75 people in Gloucester and had about 20 regular attendees at quarterly lunches (I have long held the theory that no matter the size of your community, 20 people get into everything) who produced a joint action plan. Let me know how you get on, I'd be very interested.

Keeping local people informed of everything that is going on is another important part of joined-up regeneration – people get very unhappy when they are kept in the dark, and have no say about their futures. And don't forget the politicians, those that make and approve policy – they can make life very interesting, supporting regeneration at one point and throwing up obstacles at others for their own vote-catching purposes, so deal cautiously (see Influencing later in this chapter). Not dull, is it?

Sectors

In regeneration, you'll need to understand the different motives and languages of each 'sector' of society, and then be prepared to explain them to each other on a regular basis. And you *will* have to explain – there is much public prejudice about private companies being totally grasping, and local government being hidebound and incompetent, all of which prevents people working together in regeneration. So here are some short-hand explanations you may find useful:

- **Public sector** – government-funded organisations with public benefit objectives, from which employees draw salaries to support their families and friends, and where they have to work to fairly strict guidelines

- **Private sector** – commercial organisations which make a profit from manufacturing, trading or providing services, from which owners and employees support their families and friends – an honourable line of work, from which of course public taxes are drawn, so *not* to be seen as a cash cow for local ideas. Companies tend to support regeneration anyway through enlightened self-interest

- **Voluntary sector** – publicly or privately supported charities and cooperative ventures from which employees draw smaller salaries (on the whole), but are happy because they see themselves helping family, friends and above all strangers more directly. These have a role in many areas of life from helping the elderly to personal counselling to tax advice

- **Community sector** – this is people, really, local residents, though there are some organisations like residents associations that are about representing people. They don't employ staff and so don't really fit into the voluntary sector, though they are often classed as voluntary sector in people's minds, not least because they're made up of volunteers!

Hope this helps. Blessed are the peacemakers …

Publicity

When carrying out regeneration, aim to spend 10% of your time on publicity of different kinds. You'll find it difficult – the last time I checked my own time, I was only achieving 3%. But unless people know what you're doing they can't catch fire and join in. Publicity shouldn't be seen as a distraction, it's a vital part of the job.

There are a wide range of publicity tools of course; check out which will reach most people:

- Media including newspapers, radio and TV, all accessed with press releases

- Websites and other social media (can be particularly good for reaching younger people, e.g. Facebook)

- Fliers and posters, can provide broader local coverage than either of the above

- Newsletters/mailing to local homes, can be costly, and needs time to update mailing lists

- Exhibitions and special events, also costly, so they need to be designed for particular audiences and made available at the right time and place for those audiences

The best kind of publicity is word of mouth – news so good that everyone tells everyone else – so some visible successes ('early wins') that you celebrate can help here.

Influencing

Time will come when you want to persuade other people to your point of view, so:

1. Do some research into what's already important to them

2. Present your proposals in the light of their own concerns

3. Choose the language (use their own words) and the mode of presentation that will have the best effect (and *don't* automatically assume a projected show from your computer is the best way of getting ideas across, especially if you don't have any useful pictures)

A particularly important time to do this will be when there are new bosses of any kind, either for you or for people you are working with. Don't assume they will have read the same material or have the same views as their predecessors. I made that mistake once and it was nearly fatal to the project.

Another thing – simply presenting your thoughts in the way they make sense to you will come across as preaching. This is all very well, and a robust introductory presentation can make people sit up and take notice, but it may not be so effective on a continuous basis – you don't like people always telling you the same thing, do you?

Preaching can inspire other people, but not *all* other people, so be careful you don't end up by diminishing your credibility and thereby reducing your capacity to get things done. (And if you *must* say it, write a book or an article – that only says it once!)

Negotiating

Two things to avoid, like two rocks either side of a boat – don't automatically drop your first offer, and forget any Hollywood notions of visibly shafting the other side.

If you're not a natural negotiator (or if the matter is complex), it may help you to prepare by charting the following:

- What would be your most favourable outcome over the matter in hand, and what would be your lowest acceptable position, below which you would walk away?

- Similarly, what do you think would suit the other side best, and what might be their sticking point or points?

This hopefully will map out some middle ground where you can find a mutually acceptable solution. (Of course, if there is no middle ground, save your breath, and go and find another way.)

One example of a successful negotiation was persuading the owner of a derelict warehouse to give the community a 10-year rent-free lease in exchange for renovating the building, as it was easier for the community to find capital grants than revenue grants.

This was a win–win and pretty straightforward, but do ask for advice in trickier matters, while being careful about employing experts – they can be very good, but may come out with bold statements in the middle of negotiations and only tell you the reasons afterwards, which can be somewhat alarming!

One tricky situation is a complex partnership project with several stakeholders that takes time to come to fruition. Your research into other stakeholders' objectives and sticking points will be vital, and need to be continuously refreshed as circumstances change, otherwise what you think has been agreed may mysteriously change. It ain't over till it's over – and take particular care that your own colleagues continue to support your position, or you may end up feeling rather lonely.

And one last thing – always be very clear with everyone what you are negotiating about, and what each side is saying. Be pedantic about agreeing and noting the position at the beginning and end of every meeting. You don't want any embarrassing postscripts or delays due to misunderstandings.

Conflict

I make first contact with people very pleasantly, and I start from the assumption that they will naturally give me information to help the local regeneration effort in the same way that I would give them any help they need. This seems to work.

My earliest charm offensives were around being nice to school dinner ladies in the hope of getting larger platefuls – it was a good basic policy, though I'm now fat – but what I call the 'favourite nephew' approach may not be for you. Whatever approach you take, the more people you deal with in complex situations the more your own character will be revealed to others, so (while I'm not suggesting you be other than yourself) be aware of how you come across.

With the best will in the world, however, people will disagree and occasionally fall out. If this interferes with your regeneration objectives you will want to help heal the rift, probably by speaking to the two sides separately in the first instance rather than going straight for a reconciliation meeting. If you don't know what to do about a situation, maybe this is a sign that someone else needs to be brought in to solve it, so look for that person.

This is particularly true of course if the conflict involves you personally. An early meeting with the other party is best – don't leave things to fester. If it's really bad, you may want somebody with you at the meeting, or to be the peacemaker between the two of you. Of course, a policy of 'covering your back' may seem attractive, so that other people take responsibility for everything, but I'm assuming that you as the local regeneration worker want to be the catalyst that takes things forward, and you can't be a good catalyst if you're not in the front line looking forwards.

Leadership

There are a number of basic styles, taught me some years ago, which the same leader can use in different situations:

- **Telling** – giving someone clear and unambiguous instructions ('I say to a man, Go, and he goeth')
- **Selling** – encouraging someone to do something, leaving them to decide some of the detail
- **Partnering** – doing something alongside someone
- **Delegating** – stating the objective and leaving them to carry on

There are also many textbooks and courses on leadership, but only one dedication – to the people you are leading. If you don't have the courage of your convictions, you'll be convicted in your absence, *but* remember, no ego trips, or you'll end up only leading yourself (see Vanity Regeneration, Chapter 3).

> Level 5 leaders display a powerful mixture of personal humility and indomitable will. They're incredibly ambitious, but their ambition is first and foremost for the cause, for the organization and its purpose, not themselves.
>
> (Jim Collins (2001), *Good to Great (2001)*, 21st century AD)

When the best leaders have done their work, the people say, we did it ourselves.

> (Lao Tse, *Tao Te Ching*, 4th century BC)

People Management

If you are managing a group of any kind, simply treat others as you'd wish to be treated yourself. You'll be amazed.

Justice is very important in people management, and do-as-you-would-be-done-by is the simplest justice there is.

As with leadership (which is a related skill but a wider issue), there are many people management books to choose from, find the one that suits you best – my own favourites are in Further Reading at the end of this chapter.

Incidentally, speaking of people's motivation, you might be interested in a theory developed by Douglas McGregor in his book *The Human Side of Enterprise* (1960), who suggested that people's behaviour is determined by unsatisfied needs that they want to satisfy. These needs can be put in a hierarchy, or order of priority from the top:

1. Physiological needs, e.g. food

2. Personal safety

3. Social belonging

4. Self-esteem

5. Personal reputation

6. Self-fulfilment, i.e. development to one's potential

The last three are rarely fully satisfied, so may well be on the mind of people you are working with.

(Based on McGregor, Douglas *The Human Side of Enterprise* (1960) pp. 35–9 © McGraw-Hill Education and reproduced with permission.)

Fun

'If it don't bring delight, it ain't right.'
    I can't remember who told me that, but particularly for any activity involving volunteers, at least 50% of the time must be about enjoyment.
    What are you planning for the rest of your life?
    See what I mean?

> One local community environment group, down to only four members, put out a simple plea for volunteers for weekly work days on site. That was the need, but the message translated starkly as 'we want people for regular hard physical labour' – so they got no takers, and also missed out on people that could have made refreshments on the day to make it all more enjoyable, and who could have brought in their fitter friends and relatives to help on site.

Volunteers

If you're a volunteer, you want to be treated with respect as freely giving of your spare time. If you're a paid person working with volunteers, remember this, and while being clear about roles and responsibilities for everyone's benefit, and treating volunteers as equals, don't make the mistake of treating them as your employees. We're all in this together, but there are some niceties to be observed.

Whoever you are, be prepared for a turnover of volunteers, for the best of reasons – health issues, house move, volunteering for something else – and so whatever you're doing must give people satisfaction, and be seen to be satisfying so more people join in. The chance of any learning or training opportunities through volunteering is a plus. Fun is good too – at least 50% of the time must be enjoyable to ensure a vibrant community organisation. Volunteers also have different gifts – find something for everyone, and they'll bring their friends.

Connections

In regeneration, as in many fields, there is a vital link between energy and expertise in order to get things done.

In regeneration, this link is fuelled by information about gaps in meeting local needs, and also by information about new opportunities to meet those needs.

'Excellence' equals 'Making a difference' powered by these 'Two types of Connection'.

$E = MC^2$ (sorry about that).

For example, in order to be financially sustainable, a new neighbourhood resource centre needed paying tenants for two-thirds of the building to support community activity in the other third. A doctor's surgery needed new top-quality space for which it was prepared to pay top price – the connection suited both parties so well it became the cornerstone of the whole development.

So start connecting ... and the resulting synergy will be particularly valuable in times of shortage of cash. See the matrix in Appendix 2 of different English organisations by sector against the different legs of sustainable development to give you a start.

Case Study: Cinderford Partnership

In terms of an example of public/private/voluntary/community sector partnerships, there are over 1,000 to choose from among the projects funded by the UK government in the 20 years from 1990 to 2010. This example is from my own experience, the Cinderford Partnership funded by the government's Single Regeneration Budget, which ran from 1996 to 2001 in Cinderford, an ex-mining town of around 10,000 population in the Forest of Dean, Gloucestershire.

(Continued)

(Continued)

Local places which could show evidence of 'deprivation' against the government indicators were invited to bid for funding for a proposed regeneration programme. As in many places, the Cinderford bid was put together under the auspices of the local planning authority, in this case the Forest of Dean District Council, by an outside consultant with expertise in community planning and community development. The bid also had to show match funding from other partners, and proposed an ambitious programme which required over £4m of government funding.

The eventual offer from government was for £1.2m, matched by a further £1.4m from other public sector partners plus an estimated £4.3m leveraged in from the private sector and other sources. The District Council was to be the 'accountable body' and manage the actual cash, with guidance from government officers. For each of the five years there had to be an action plan which also recorded budget expenditure, and there were quarterly progress reports to the Government Office for the South West.

As part of this process, there had to be a partnership board of all interested parties, and a smaller implementation group to meet more regularly, whose first proposed members were:

- Cinderford Town Council (2 seats)
- Forest of Dean District Council as accountable body (2 seats)
- Two representatives of local business
- Gloucestershire Rural Community Council
- Gloucestershire Training and Enterprise Council (TEC)
- Royal Forest of Dean College

This group was intended to have monthly meetings, but as reports to the Government Office had to be made quarterly, then quarterly meetings became more important, when members of the wider partnership board attended, including:

- County Economic Development Department (in the process of merging with the old Gloucestershire Development Agency to eventually form 'Gloucestershire First')
- Cinderford Artspace
- CANDI youth project

All this was set up before I arrived, though I was the one who had to make it work and report to everyone regularly! These were the days before everyone had their own email address – I'd only recently taken a short course in word processing myself, having started my computing work in the late 1970s with punched cards ... so as I recall, partners received a lot of printed reports by 'snail mail'.

The only local group that weren't represented when I arrived was local churches, so Churches Together in Cinderford got added to the board. The local

Church of England vicar attended a couple of meetings as the group's representative, though nobody really took his place when he moved to another town.

I won't say that there weren't controversies along the way, as we had a good range of people not afraid to speak their minds (much better than smouldering in silence!), and occasional new representatives from partner organisations brought in fresh perspectives, but the team grew to four members of staff, and we achieved a lot between us, including:

- Shopfront painting scheme to brighten up the town centre (an early win)

- Hanging baskets scheme for the town centre

- New covered market in the town centre (see 'before' and 'after' pictures below)

Cinderford Triangle 23 July 1996 – shops and pubs had been removed many years before in order to widen the main road

Cinderford Triangle on market day 16 June 2017 – covered market delivered by the regeneration scheme

(Continued)

(Continued)

- The first ever 'Welcome to Cinderford' road signs (now being updated)

- Promotional leaflets for Cinderford

- Promotional brochure for the industrial estate

- Roadside map of firms on the industrial estate, to direct delivery drivers

- A new Enterprise Centre with its own managing board, housing the College's engineering apprentice workshops as well as 'Meals on Wheels'

- A new workspace building on the industrial estate

- New social housing replacing old apartment blocks

- Linear Park Environment Volunteers improving old railway land between the town and the Forest

After three years, as I was thinking about moving on to my next job, Mark Cunningham came into my office with a costed plan for renovating the old Palace Cinema, which had been closed for over 30 years. I advised him to present his plans to the District Council to ensure they got behind him, and that worked too – the cinema has since gone on from strength to strength.

The refurbished Palace Cinema

Further Reading

Carnegie, Dale (1936) *How to Win Friends and Influence People*. New York: Simon & Schuster – an old text that's still worth a read – for example, life is easier if you learn people's names.

Townsend, Robert (1970) *Up The Organisation*. London: Michael Joseph – also a Coronet paperback edition published in 1971 – see the section on 'People' which talks about how we are motivated to work, and the appendix about assessing your boss as a leader, which you may find a useful checklist for how to behave when leading a group.

Morris, Michael J. (1988) *The First Time Manager*. London: Kogan Page – one of many management books, but one I found most useful when I first became a manager myself.

3
Words of Warning

As soon as you start involving other people, you will come across a range of difficulties, because humans are like that. It's not too soon to list some particular regeneration pitfalls to avoid.

Due Diligence

Never assume.

There can be several difficulties when managing a regeneration programme for other people:

- Is everyone really committed to the objectives of the programme? This may be broadly true in terms of the partner organisations, but key individuals may have their own agendas, and in some cases may be wedded to alternative regeneration objectives and approaches from other initiatives – and newcomers to partner organisations may bring different ideas as well.

- Do an existing regeneration framework and recent progress reports indicate good management in place? 'Tain't necessarily so – check there is continuity between the original plan and the people now producing the reports, and that all parts of the plan are still linked to each other and working well.

- Do people who hire staff for a particular role necessarily understand that role themselves? Again, not always so, they may be hiring *you* for the expertise after all – you may need to get their attention to appreciate and agree plans for the regeneration programme as it develops (as well as being clear about their own roles), and you may need to have a strategy to keep meetings focused on the way ahead.

I would say it's better and safer to take an open view on every occasion, which of course takes some extra time, and ensure you have top-level management and political support from partners before coming in strong to give direction on the way ahead. This is possibly the most important lesson in this book – do your research – check things out before you make a move. Before you make a mistake that can't be rectified.

Experts

> 'X' is an unknown quantity, and a spurt is a drip under pressure.
>
> I heard that at school, actually, but what's the answer?

Always make sure you fully understand what experts and consultants are saying to you – hire them for their clarity above all – and get a second opinion whenever you can. Not every so-called expert is scrupulous about involving you in the detail, and some may even gloss over their own backgrounds as well as the research they have done for you – double-check the basis for any recommendations they make.

> I still bear the scars of a failed building purchase where the expert's business plan was fatally flawed. Though the whole floor area of the building was used when calculating the rental returns needed to complete the purchase, at so much per annum per square foot, it was not explained how the reception area and corridor 'rent' was going to be recovered from the tenants of the small offices.
>
> I know now how this can be done (divide your costs by the lettable space only), but I didn't then. I spotted the flaw too late. It gave me no consolation that the 20 other people who had looked at the plan hadn't spotted it either, and the building purchase failed with the loss of our (publicly funded) deposit. So be warned.

One-shot Solutions

Beware of one-shot solutions, but there is good news.

As the newly-appointed regeneration officer for the market town of Cinderford in the Forest of Dean, I was besieged by people with one-shot solutions, along the lines of 'all you need to do is this, and the town will be regenerated'. Proposed solutions included:

- A new 50-bed hotel (never materialised – and there was already an underused 44-bed hotel in the next village)

- A new major supermarket (also didn't happen – there were two supermarkets in the town already, with a third cut-price store about to open, though local desire for something new may still triumph 20 years later)

- Replacing town centre shops on the open space created by road widening some 40 years before (this was achieved in a small way, though to some controversy)

What was the good news? People were clearly thinking about change for the better, and we achieved a lot together in five years, as noted in Chapter 2, including a new covered market area, shopfront improvements, town signposting and industrial estate promotion, new housing, an improved local park and a reopened cinema.

I'm all for making a complex problem as simple as possible, but if it is complex – and towns usually are – then be prepared for several 'solutions', not just one.

Fashion

Fashion and sustainability are enemies.

In the 1960s, big shopping malls and ring roads were held to be the answer to town regeneration. Now we know they weren't, not for the long term anyway, but look how many towns in the UK took that approach.

So be very sure that any new ideas you may be following have staying power. No country can afford total regeneration of all its settlements every 20 years.

How can we be sure? Check your evidence base! Ask local residents, and study good practice in similar places before you decide, but remember that regenerating each place in its own image – not blind copycatting – is much more likely to produce a longer-lasting outcome. Build on local strengths, not fashionable ideas.

Great Expectations

People will want it all to happen tomorrow.

There is a balancing act in managing expectations. You want people to be enthused about the outcomes of regeneration, but then you need to tell them enough about the practicalities to stop them chasing you for results daily, and without telling them so much detail that it dampens their enthusiasm totally!

Don't forget to be honest, particularly when answering direct questions – any squirming on your part will be very visible – but spend some time thinking which of your audience will be interested in particular parts of the picture, and make sure you keep them up to date accordingly.

Eureka Moment

Classically these occur when one individual has an inspiration based on only three apparently connected ideas or pieces of information, and builds a whole initiative on this basis alone. What I call (with some irony) a 'jolly good idea'.

> There once was a grant scheme for suburban neighbourhood centres, and one of the successful bidders matched the scheme criteria to a notoriously deprived area of the city, which had a lot of old houses turned into bed-sits, and linked the tenants' health needs to a redevelopment of the nearby health centre to include new housing - Eureka!
>
> £40,000 of feasibility study later it was clear that not only was this area *not* the most deprived part of the city, but that the proposed redevelopment needed £5m support from the local health trust which was not remotely on the cards - and they nearly lost the original funding.

So beware of 'eureka moments', they are liable to lead to a wrong turning, and occasionally to disaster. In this case, happily, another site was found and the health centre went with the project, so all was not lost. Second moral – don't give up.

Third moral – if you *think* you've got a 'eureka moment' on your hands, then check it out quickly, or partners may become restive ...

Siren Song

You're caught up in a beautiful melody. Someone is singing your song, and you're convinced they've got the rights of it, and are on your side.

Dash of cold water. Are you still sure? Ask yourself, are they sharing your risk, or are they getting something else out of it all, and you're actually dancing to someone else's agenda? Get a perspective from someone you trust.

> It's useful anyway to find an independent professional mentor if you can. I knew I needed such a person to support me on the Oxfordshire programme, but I couldn't find one in the county. I should have gone back to a Bristol colleague who had already given me good advice, but I'd become too caught up to think outside the box and remember him. Damn.

More difficult is how to deal with a partner who is clearly under the influence of someone else's siren song. You can't persuade them of this – try and find ways that allow them to persuade themselves – find another singer, or someone they trust.

Knee-jerk Reactions

I am deeply suspicious of knee-jerk reactions, as by their nature they ignore some of the facts, and are first (and simpler) cousins to a 'Eureka moment'.

> For example, any local design issue will inevitably cause someone to suggest a schools competition. My response would be, 'Would you ask primary school children to redesign and redecorate your own home?' Well then. Involve everyone in planning the future by all means – and so you should – but don't confuse inspiration with delivery.

We'd all love to be known as flair players, but better to think it through than shoot from the hip. And remember – flair players tend to be choosing from a play-book of what they already know is possible, they're not guessing, they're just a little swifter at making the connections. But better to take your own time – we want long-standing results, not first impressions.

Understanding

Whenever we come across something large and complex we don't understand, we tend to:

a. Focus on a bit we *do* understand, and

b. It's a bit we understand but don't like.

Everybody does this, it seems to be a natural reaction, and it explains a lot about people objecting to change.

On the positive side, as we learn more, we want to understand more quickly, and seek shorthand summaries of the ultimate truth.

For example, when developing the Regeneration Framework for Gloucester, we seemed to go through a succession of touchstone phrases, including 'cafe culture' and 'light industry' (I wish I'd written them all down, there were so many). This also seems to be part of the process.

Not everybody wants to understand everything about regeneration, of course, some will settle for what they see as a practical level of knowledge and stick there. Your best plan as a regeneration worker is to say you're learning all the time (no one likes a clever clogs), keep a genuinely open mind, and people will keep giving you parts of the puzzle. Remember, it's meant to be complex.

Clever Clogs

Every now and then a message will come about a brilliant new solution, based on a new approach or new information.

Great! So how does it work?

Let's be fair, there is such a thing as innovation, and the fact that many messengers can't describe the new thing accurately doesn't mean it's no good. Check it out, if only to make sure that it isn't just a fashionable approach that only works in certain circumstances.

I was once assured that privatised railway companies would produce much-needed investment in the UK railway system. This didn't happen – train services stayed privatised but the rail network itself was taken back into public ownership – and the messenger changed his views. Mind you, the UK government seems to be trying this approach again ...

In the aftermath of the credit crunch of 2008, there was a renewed focus on something called tax increment financing (TIF), or 'accelerated development zones' (ADZ) in the UK. Instead of government funding, private investors put cash into development schemes, and are repaid by taxes from new businesses in the development that would otherwise go to government. This sounds plausible, but a bit like the railway story – let's see if it works in practice in a few pilot areas.

So accept the good news by all means, but don't abandon faith in your own assessments – and make sure you know what you're talking about, too! I am reminded that if you point a finger at somebody, three fingers are pointing back at you (a very salutary note for a book author, too).

Vanity Regeneration

Do you dream of yourself opening a brand new building, or being pulled modestly from behind the crowd to have your virtues extolled?

Danger sign – regeneration is about people, not about you.

Keep those dreams of big ribbons and monumental buildings away from your mind (that is, if you must have them at all) – and be wary of anyone who talks about 'landmark structures'. I can personally recommend quiet satisfaction – but *after* the job is done, not as an objective in itself.

I once had a perfect moment.

It was about 10 o'clock at night, and I'd just come out of a seeing a film at the newly-refurbished and reopened Palace Cinema in Cinderford.

I stopped on the corner by Chris Hughes' cafe with its newly-painted mural of local mining history, and looked across to my old regeneration project offices, then occupied by a much-needed women and children's clothing shop. Beyond that I could see the newly-extended Co-op supermarket, straight across the road was the old Swan pub being done up, and I knew that just down the road was the new outdoor covered market we'd put up on the Triangle in the town centre.

Magic.

And don't forget, the bigger or fancier the development, the more you need to be sure it will last despite any potential changes in climate, economy or power supply. 'My name is Ozymandias, King of Kings – look on my works, ye mighty, and despair' – but the statue's head was broken in the sand (Percy Bysshe Shelley, 'Ozymandias', 1818).

The Pits

This is the lowest point in the book.

Some dreams will die.

Not everyone is a nice person either.

Case Study: Four Gates Centre, Gloucester

How can you lose £3m funding given in good faith by a Government grant scheme? By the ground changing under your feet, as this case study shows, though there are other lessons to be learnt as well.

I joined Gloucester City Council in February 2004 as a Community Strategy Officer, with the specific task of taking on the project management of a new neighbourhood centre for the centre of Gloucester funded by something called the Building Communities Scheme – a Government initiative that was providing the £3m. At the same time as this project was developing, the Gloucester Heritage Urban Regeneration Company (GHURC) was starting work with an initial allocation of £20m of Government backing via the South West Regional Development Agency (SWRDA) on a much wider range of developments to improve a number of key sites in the city.

There were some communication tasks from the outset as the neighbourhood centre project was very much a public sector proposal for community benefit, rather than being led by local people themselves. Happily, another officer in the Community Strategy team was already supporting the development of local community partnerships around Gloucester, and the growth of the City Centre Community Partnership (CCCP) became closely linked with the neighbourhood centre project – in fact, the name 'Four Gates Centre' was coined by a CCCP member as reflecting the four 'gate' streets (Eastgate, Southgate, Westgate and Northgate) that meet in the middle of the city.

As well as local residents, the local health centre had an interest in the new neighbourhood centre as a base to replace their ageing premises and 1960s portakabins, and I quickly found other interested parties including local businesses. Encouraged by the local spirit of redevelopment, I walked round the whole city centre and identified a number of sites that might possibly do for the Four Gates Centre. I then gave the list to all the identified interest groups and encouraged them to look for themselves and make their recommendations. After totting up the scores, it was clear that the overall preferred site – not least for the health centre, who didn't want to move too far from their existing patients – was part of a college campus selected for redevelopment as one of the seven major sites ('the Magnificent Seven') earmarked for improvement by GHURC, subsequently referred to as the Greyfriars Quarter.

We developed a business plan approved by the project steering group, with the health centre as core tenant and a range of planned community services including training courses to meet local employment needs. So far so good – and at this point (2005 – the GHURC Regeneration Framework was formally launched in 2006), we were riding high.

Most of the college site was planned for new housing (the college itself was moving to the docks) with the neighbourhood centre to be placed in a corner of the new development, facing the city museum. The Homes & Communities Agency (HCA – previously English Partnerships, who had acquired the site from the college to enable the college to move to the docks) put out tenders for a housing developer whose task would include the building of the Four Gates Centre with the Building Communities funding. Two firms were shortlisted, and one of them given the job.

In August 2008 the chosen firm declared insolvency. Months and months of discussion between the Four Gates Centre steering group led by local people and the developer went down the drain, and discussions started all over again as the HCA turned to the second firm on the shortlist, rather than re-tender. About this time the Building Communities fund (which had always had a spending deadline) became subsumed into the GHURC's pot from SWRDA, so control of the money effectively devolved to the GHURC board made up of 23 people from the public, private and voluntary sectors.

(Continued)

(Continued)

The HCA and the new firm in consultation with GHURC and the city council had many things to agree as well as the details of building the neighbourhood centre, and the discussions took ages. I don't know all the reasons why it took years to get to contract signing – I wasn't senior enough to be a member of the relevant working group – but by the time the deal was done, an axe had fallen on the GHURC funding. Government grants were being cut, as part of the proposed abolition of SWRDA, and the GHURC was told there would only be £10m available and no more.

By this time the Four Gates Centre steering group – now incorporated as the Westgate Community Trust in anticipation of running the completed building – had realised that the GHURC had so many other things on their plate that there was a danger of the Four Gates Centre being forgotten. A campaign was launched to re-present the project, with the first campaign targets being GHURC officers, one of whom started referring to the Four Gates Centre as the 'jewel in the crown'. A site visit was organised to a similar neighbourhood centre in nearby Cheltenham, but in the end only one member of the GHURC board – the local Gloucester Member of Parliament, Parmjit Dhanda – came to see it, and he simply said 'We want one'.

Parmjit however was only one of 23 people on the board, and at the critical meeting in 2009, despite a presentation by the chair of the Westgate Community Trust, three other projects were preferred ahead of the Four Gates Centre, including a walkway scheme connecting the city centre to the flagship Gloucester Quays project a good half mile away. I had left the City Council by then, and so was not able to carry out my usual task of briefing the voluntary sector member on the board (could the walkway scheme be delivered for less while still delivering the Four Gates Centre?), who consequently had nothing to add to the presentation. And while efforts continued to be made, the dream died.

June 2014 – Houses going up on the Four Gates Centre site

What else could we have done? Nothing through the chain of command, as the GHURC board held the overall responsibility for delivering the regeneration programme and levering in private and public investment, whilst the site remained in the ownership of one of its core members, HCA. I could have made myself unpopular (see Unpopularity in Chapter 12) by going above people's heads to local elected councillors, but who knows whether that would have made a difference. The City Centre Community Partnership had become somewhat divorced from the Westgate Community Trust, so there was no popular local groundswell to raise a protest – perhaps there's even a lesson there about the need for the community to own and lead community projects from the outset.

If only the housing negotiations had proceeded more swiftly, and the original developer had not gone bust, there would be a training and health-based centre we could visit that had been doing great things by, with and for the people of Gloucester city centre for the past many years. There were more twists and turns in the story to come, but thanks partly to pressure from the City Centre Community Partnership, the good news is the housing developer is now, in 2017, building a smaller community centre on the site (200 sq m with apartments above, but without the health centre).

Incidentally, the community ownership idea is underscored by the success of another Building Communities project, the Victoria Park Community Centre in Bridgwater, Somerset. The lead officer Nicola Slawski notes that this project succeeded because of the strong partnership between Sedgemoor District Council (for whom she worked, and owners of the original site), community leaders and other agencies, particularly the Somerset Coast Primary Care Trust who helped secure significant additional funding (a doctor's surgery was also a feature of this project). The willingness of the partnership to fight for the original vision when funding problems could have watered down the scheme was another factor in its success.

The community were involved from the start, it was their passion which convinced the authorities to select the Victoria Park project as the recommended Building Communities scheme from Somerset, and their representative organisation Newtown & Victoria Springboard Ltd have managed the centre for many years and signed a 125-year lease with Sedgemoor District Council in October 2016.

Further Reading

Maliphant, Andrew (2014) 'Power to the people: Putting community into urban regeneration', *Journal of Urban Regeneration and Renewal*, 8(1): 86–100, Henry Stewart Publications – an article with more detail on the Four Gates Centre within the social regeneration of Gloucester city centre.

4
Cross-cutting Issues

Whatever we're trying to achieve, some factors just keep finding their way in, not least those that relate to the physical environment.

Sustainable Development

> I make no apologies for continually raising this issue, as repetition is the father of learning. My grandfather's view was 'say what you're going to say, say it, and then say what you've said' – and he *was* a professional preacher.

Sustainable development has become a bit of a weasel phrase, used by the UK government to justify new planning policies, but it is intended to be the key to making sure that the changes we make are universally good news.

One smart-guy definition of sustainable development would be the action necessary to achieve sustainable communities, but that doesn't take us forward in practice.

A useful guide for many years has been the 'three-legged stool' of sustainable development, with physical, social and economic legs.

This can give us some practical tests for proposed new ventures, for example:

- Will they protect the environment, using renewable physical resources and causing no long-term damage?

- Will they be financially viable, and show good value-for-money for their set-up costs?

- Will they engage and support the local community who will then provide human support in the long term?

Questions along these lines can be included in project appraisal, for example, and we are getting more definitive best practice, such as:

- Hard guidelines on how to build environmentally-friendly and secure buildings

- A range of initiatives to control the environmental impact of the motor car

- Ways to assess your 'carbon footprint' – the net amount of harmful carbon dioxide your activities produce

- More ways to recycle materials

The sustainability debate is not just about the environment however. There are beginning to be concerns about the health implications of potential population movements as the result of climate change – do you expect a future influx of climate refugees in your area? This might affect your forward planning. There may need to be an international economic solution to the destruction of the Brazilian rain forests, or excessive fishing around the world, so who knows what costly solutions may be necessary to stop bad environmental practice at the local level, such as paying people to recycle their cars (the UK government's recent 'scrappage' scheme).

Rather than a fattened environmental 'leg' for the sustainable development stool, which is a common view, I would argue climate change is arguably now a fourth leg – and a wobbly one – that is affecting all the other three. The goalposts for sustainable development that we thought we were identifying may now be very moveable, and it will be important to keep abreast of the latest wisdom as the context for regeneration is still changing. 'Think globally, act locally' was never more true.

Environment

'The environment' is the subject of a lot of talk these days, but remember there are many layers:

- The 'green' environment – trees, meadows, ponds and other wildlife habitats; agricultural land

- The 'built' environment – human-made structures and buildings

- The atmosphere – weather patterns and air quality

Climate change is justifiably getting a lot of the attention, but don't forget that local places where people live are also 'the environment', and make sure you address all aspects of that in your regeneration programme.

One important reminder is that 'green' does not necessarily equal 'natural'. We may be used to seeing well-manicured public parks with water features, flowers and trees, but these are not suitable habitats for the wealth of wild creatures and plants that would be there if people were not involved. Ducks can also make a right mess of artificial urban ponds.

Throwing garden rubbish into the countryside on the basis it is all 'green' is also not a good idea, as some overseas plants have taken root and changed local habitats forever – just mention 'Japanese knotweed' to countryside rangers in the UK and watch their faces change colour ...

Climate Change

The Intergovernmental Panel on Climate Change (IPCC) is the leading international body for the assessment of climate change, established by the United Nations Environment Programme and the World Meteorological Organization in 1988. Among their publications is a graph (see Figure 4.1) that shows the rising levels of carbon in the atmosphere, with all that means for global warming, changing weather patterns and ambient temperatures. Whether or not wholly caused by humans – the IPCC report considers the increase is largely due to the burning of fossil fuels – the concern has to be at what point (due to increased growth rates perhaps) will the graph move sharply upwards beyond the point of no return?

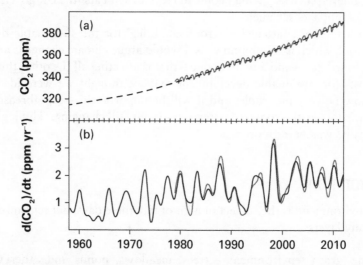

Figure 4.1   (a) Globally averaged CO_2 dry-air mole fractions from Scripps Institution of Oceanography (SIO) at monthly time resolution based on measurements from Mauna Loa, Hawaii and South Pole (red) and NOAA/ESRL/GMD at quasi-weekly time resolution (blue). SIO values are deseasonalized. (b) Instantaneous growth rates for globally averaged atmospheric CO_2 using the same colour code as in (a). Growth rates are calculated as the time derivative of the deseasonalized global averages (Dlugokencky et al., 1994)

In this version black lines denote red, and grey lines denote blue in the original.

(IPCC, 2014: 167)

There are other pollutants as well, such as methane (from cows), and nitrous oxide and other gases from motor cars, that also increase warming. Yes, we can all go to Mars.

We have seen a growing response to the challenge of climate change and its implications, and some actions are becoming commonplace, for example:

• The search for low energy solutions (80% of global warming is about energy, one way or another), including piping heat from power stations to nearby housing

- Efforts to reduce the number of polluting motor cars

- Research into different agricultural solutions (much of the remaining 20% of the issue)

There are some things like turning off lights that are classically domestic actions, and some like the proposal to capture solar energy in the Sahara Desert that are rather more global and strategic. What about the middle-level actions to include in regeneration plans?

There are two main approaches to be researched and applied:

1. **'Mitigation'** – building things that have minimal effect on the environment in general and carbon levels in particular, have low energy use and take up fewer resources

2. **'Adaptation'** – preparing the built environment for expected changes in the climate in future, such as rising flood levels and warmer temperatures

The standards for these two approaches will probably change as the planet changes, so check them out – the 2010 version of the UK Code for Sustainable Homes, for example, was withdrawn by the UK Government in 2015 and has been succeeded by revised guidance under other titles.

There has been a campaign to get everyone to reduce their 'carbon emissions' by 10%, but only time will tell if that is enough, or indeed if that is the right approach. And let's hope we collectively find the right level of all these actions before the graph leaves us behind.

Renewable Energy

Time was when you put an electric plug in a socket and the problem was solved. Now, due to environmental concerns, there are a growing number of renewable energy options that are coming into regeneration, for example:

- Heat pumps – drawing power from a heat exchange with the air or the earth – air is better for urban areas

- Wind turbines – no good in urban areas where the wind is too variable. Can be good on the coast, but are more expensive to place out at sea

- Tidal energy – definitely one for the coast, and a lot of research is taking place into effective ways to harness the natural power that moves seawater four times a day

- Solar power – converting the sun's rays into energy, such as solar voltaic panels providing illumination at rural bus stops, or even direct heating of domestic water supplies

- Biofuels – burning wood chips or other renewable matter, such as methane from sewage farms, rather than 'fossil fuel' oil and coal that are going to run out eventually, and release large amounts of CO_2 anyway

The London Borough of Merton started a trend by requiring new developments to produce 10% of their own power, and it is becoming commonplace to make renewable energy provision part of the requirement for larger regeneration schemes, so this is another aspect of change to take on board.

Nuclear energy is sometimes added to the list of energy options, though it's not a renewable source as I'm told known world supplies of uranium will run out in 60 years or so. Nuclear power stations as structures also have a limited life, and the waste has to be put somewhere safe for 100,000 years. Nuclear power stations are said by their supporters to be the 'cleanest' in terms of the environment (are there failsafe measures that click in automatically when there are no people about?), but are probably not a viable option at the local level.

While we're on national issues, I'm told Denmark has invested heavily in off-shore wind turbines, and has a reciprocal deal with Norway to share the benefits of Norwegian hydroelectric power when the wind is not blowing. This leads me to expect energy sharing at more regional and local levels in the future.

Another trend from the Transition movement is an 'energy descent plan' – how can we prepare to deal with less oil- and coal-based power at a local level, and make a positive virtue of it? Kinsale in Ireland produced such a plan in 2005, and another was completed for Totnes in Devon in 2013. This is not just about local energy production, but about reviewing *all* aspects of local life against a positive vision of a future using less energy, and is another example of how local people can take control of what might be thought purely national issues.

Water

There is good news, and there is bad news.

The good news is that water is a necessity of life, and so there is a wealth of knowledge about how to obtain and supply it. The UK in particular is a green and pleasant land (and consequently very popular for current and probably future immigration).

The bad news is too much or too little water, floods in some areas and droughts in others, partly a product of local geography. This is not just about the natural landscape though – the 2007 floods in Gloucester were not about the river rising, but the drains in the city not being able to cope with unusually high rainfall.

So 'sustainable urban drainage' is one issue to look out for. Floods can also spread pollution such as sewage to other bodies of water. As ever, there may be some added value to find – any new engineering works in your area may be able to solve some other local issues, such as better access roads, cycle paths and footpaths along the lines of new flood defences.

Geologists, meteorologists and civil engineers can help you with all of this. If you find them on the seashore looking worried, ask them how high the water will rise when the ice caps melt, and set your building plans accordingly. If you find them in the desert looking worried, ask them how long to the solution ...

On the subject of water shortages, there is now something called 'grey water', i.e. not suitable for drinking, but fine for some other purposes, such as using old bath water to flush toilets. This needs some engineering, but can be very helpful in water conservation, and takes some of the weight off water purification plants. How about rainwater collection for every household lucky enough to have rain?

Peak Oil

I was asked what I thought about peak oil at a job interview - I hadn't heard of it, thought it sounded like some sort of quality assurance method. Anyway, I didn't get the job (lesson - keep up to date in your chosen profession!).

Peak oil is the point at which the demand for fossil fuel and its by-products (which includes modern computers) exceeds supply. There is debate about the timing of this – there are peak oil deniers just as there are climate change deniers, while some say we have already reached peak oil – but there is more agreement that a world whose economy, transport and communications have become dependent on the supply of oil will have to make changes if the supply of said oil is reduced (this of course is one of the strategic concerns that continues to focus the Western world on the Middle East).

There seem to be two main responses to peak oil:

1. **'Business as usual'** – a determination to continue to find new sources of supply, including artificial oil, in order to keep the world in its current shape – and so what if the price of oil goes up? The counter-argument is that this is a short-sighted view, that we would be better investing in alternative energy production and markets, and that anyway some of the desperate searches for new oil will release more gases that contribute to climate change

2. **'Energy descent'** – active planning for a time when oil will indeed become scarce, and making this a positive approach to change by gradually adapting rather than taking the risk of a sudden crisis – a recent lorry drivers strike in the UK reminded people that in a highly-sophisticated society we can be only three days away from food shortages. The counter-argument is that this view is unnecessarily alarmist, as the global economy is designed to deal with variations in oil supply as any other market condition (Hopkins, 2008)

You will make up your own mind about where the truth lies, but in terms of local regeneration and looking to a secure future, it seems to me that maximising local self-sufficiency in energy, food production, transport and communications – and jobs – is a sensible approach whatever the future holds.

Transport

A good transport network underpins all of regeneration, so get interested in this area too. Everyone relies on transport (even the housebound, as services need to get to them), so an otherwise good regeneration scheme could fail if the transport network is not capable of supporting it.

There are some basic elements, of course:

- People or things that need to travel, or be transported

- Modes of transport – everything from trains, boats and planes to lorries, private cars, public buses, bikes and feet. (These modes are not all equal – for example, however people arrive in your area, they will walk, or be wheeled, once they arrive, so pedestrian facilities are a critical part to get right.)

- Routes for travel – roads, rivers, airways

As well as understanding the needs and requirements for all of these, transport planning and traffic management, get into the connections between different modes – links between airports and buses is a classic – and also dealing with the impact of too many users – traffic calming, bus and cycle lanes, pedestrianised areas, congestion charging for popular destinations, and so on. Get the local transport plan from the relevant authority for a grasp of the wider transport context for your area.

The environmental debate also has a big part to play, due to the harmful emissions of car exhausts. Encouraging cycling is also seen as good for local health, and increasingly we are seeing 20 mph speed limits in urban areas, which is a more practical way of making all transport including cycling safer than building cycle lanes (which is not always possible anyway, depending on the location).

So, it's another technical area to understand; you will need to meet local highway and transport officers, and there will be fruitful conversations along the lines of *why* and *how*:

- Why do we need more roads? (it simply encourages cars)

- Why are trains and buses not more frequent?

- How can we make it easy for people to get to work (what's the 'travel-to-work area'?), or customers to get to businesses, without making life unhealthy?

- How can we provide electric recharge ports or plug-in facilities for new electric vehicles?

- What contingencies do we have if oil-based transport comes under serious threat – are there any positive benefits of canal-based transport, for example?

There is also a question of *who* does *what*. Regeneration schemes will often involve bits of the transport network (motorways, bus and rail stations, rail tracks) that are managed by different authorities as well as by private companies – your local transport plan should give you some clues about this.

As ever, there will be synergies to find between transport work and other regeneration objectives, such as flower planting on roundabouts to make places more attractive, and wildlife areas in otherwise waste ground. Turning off street lights between midnight and 5 a.m. is also becoming more common as a way of conserving energy supplies.

Where the people aspect really comes in is around that dazzling status symbol and all-round convenience, the motor car. Everyone is in favour of fewer cars on the road, so that they themselves can drive to the shops! (I see bigger stores are going back to making home deliveries, by the way, which will help. How about banning car advertising on television?) Not everyone has cars, of course, so as well as some attention to car park environments and how people get about once they park, there is also the question of access to shops and services by public transport.

There is a view that civilisation cannot be saved by rules, but rather by self-restraint. The biggest battle is to encourage people to review their personal transport plans to reduce environmental impacts, and regeneration workers will certainly have the opportunity to spread the word about that.

Diversity

<blockquote>
Different

    Individuals

        Valuing

            Each other

                Regardless of

        Skin

      Intellect

    Talents or

Years
</blockquote>

Or regardless of any other differences, for that matter. I don't know who originally coined this definition, but the world is too diverse to label it all, be prepared for surprises.

For example, we hear a lot about facilities for young people, but did *you* do the same things between the ages of 5 and 15? There are at least three different age bands to cater for before you get to teenagers – who want 'nuffin' of course but need a space to hang out, and an approach that involves them directly. And what about older people – will they necessarily want to spend time with people 15 or more years older or younger, even if they all have grey hair like me?!

So have an eye to diversity – and if people say there isn't the money to cater for it, why not involve the people who would benefit in helping to raise the extra cash?

There are also people of course for whom 'diversity' is not just an academic topic, as they have physical issues that can inhibit them or they feel inhibit them from taking a full part in their local community. This is another field of human endeavour that is continually looking for new solutions, and you would do well to get in touch with a local campaigning organisation such as Equal Lives in Norfolk who can bring you up to date. As they say on their website:

> Equal Lives is led by people who face disabling barriers and is dedicated to making your voice heard. We support people to empower themselves to live independent lives. Our aim is to give you the support you need to live your own life and to remove disabling barriers. We are very involved in campaigning on issues that affect you to try and influence policy decisions. We're also here to provide support and information for the day to day tasks of living. Whether you need to employ a personal assistant, find out what benefits you're able to

receive or you need help or advice for caring for an elderly friend or relative we are here to help.

(Equal Lives, 2017)

Population

Setting aside controversial issues such as immigration and birth control, the chances are that wherever you are living (particularly in urban areas), there are more people than there were before the industrial revolution of the 19th century.

In the UK there are well-known pockets of unemployment due to the collapse of local industries such as mining, steel works and ship-building. If this sounds like the place you are looking to regenerate, then you will naturally have as one of your targets ways in which local people can be gainfully employed – ideally perhaps in connection with other local opportunities or issues such as food production or the response to climate change.

It may seem daunting – it probably is – but it's important to make your best efforts in this area of employing people, so that depending on how you get on, you can highlight to regional and central government their need to get involved to address any identified problems that can't be managed locally. If government won't take on people issues, of course, then people are likely to take on the government, and can find polite but effective ways to make sure they know that – the recent UK referendum vote to leave the European Union could be an example of this!

Services

Some of the things we want for our area will be new facilities, but others will be new or improved services for our community.

A good example of a service that has come under threat in the UK due to local government budget cuts is public libraries. These can actually be run very successfully by local volunteers, as was shown by the first wave of such ventures in the English county of Buckinghamshire. There is also UK legislation for the community to identify and take over such 'community assets'.

The second wave of community libraries has included counties such as Gloucestershire, where I chaired a local group who took over Mitcheldean library on 1 November 2012 as a community 'hub' managed under a new cooperative for community benefit. The running costs were subject to grant aid from the County Council, who still made savings of over £60,000 per annum on Mitcheldean library alone, and we were able to reintroduce local services like training in computers that were just disappearing from the immediate area.

Another service that has suffered under the cuts, and this time a national initiative, is 'Business Link'. In the past this UK service provided much-needed advice for people wishing to start their own business and become self-employed, very necessary in times of job losses. A pilot project in the Forest of Dean supported with county-managed training funds was then converted into a self-sustaining project, 'Forest of Dean Entrepreneurs' (see case study in Chapter 6), with sponsorship from local firms such as accountants and printers who have an interest in seeing new businesses prosper.

The critical thing in both cases was setting up an effective partnership to take the services forward – it can be done.

Planet Change

> I thought I'd coined a new phrase, but then I found a website called 'Planet Change'! Moral – be humble – the world is full of clever people.

Change on top of change – this is the most fluid part of the regeneration world. We've become familiar with the phrase 'climate change', but there are other issues too, such as what will we do when the demand for fossil fuels outstrips the supply? (The so-called peak oil – in practice this needs similar energy solutions as for climate change, as it happens.)

The whole of this area of concern is developing rapidly, and there is huge debate about what to do globally, let alone locally. It's really your responsibility as a regeneration worker ('continuous professional development') to search the Internet using new phrases like planet change to bring yourself up to date. Read the papers too, but best not the same newspaper every time, get different perspectives.

Case Study: Swansea Community Energy and Enterprise Scheme

In November 2014 the City and County of Swansea (the local council) put out a brief for consultants to work on the development of community-scale renewable energy projects.

A detailed feasibility study had confirmed that a community solar photovoltaic (PV) scheme (solar panels) was viable, and proposed that the council supported the development of a social enterprise model to develop a community-owned energy scheme on a phased basis, starting with non-domestic properties and moving on to local authority social housing. The scheme objectives were summarised as:

- Identify appropriate community-focused business models, renewable technologies and develop transferable skills and capacity within the community, to enhance the environmental, economic and social wellbeing

- Create a self-sustaining solution to permanently raise aspiration and break the trans-generational cycle of poverty

- Diversify local income by taking advantage of local renewable sources and generate long-term revenue which offers the prospect of change at community level

- Improve the comfort and utility of houses/community facilities by making them warmer, more energy efficient and more cost effective to run

- Communicate the benefits of setting up a community-scale and community-owned renewable energy project and be an exemplar for future projects

The background to this scheme was to explore how renewable energy projects could create wider social and economic value in Swansea, the idea for which came from the local Labour Party manifesto for Swansea. Similar community energy schemes around the country have tended to develop from grass roots support in the local community, this one differed in that the scheme was developed to a point by the local council in partnership with a number of local experts and community members, who were then able to operate independently from the council as a separate entity.

Chris Small was the council officer leading the project. A small number of founder directors, including Chris, set up the Swansea Community Energy and Enterprise Scheme (SCEES) in September 2015 as a registered community benefit society, run independently by a group of people from the local area including local councillor representation. The declared aim was to offer secure ethical investments in renewable energy projects and use profits from each scheme to support some of the most disadvantaged communities in Swansea.

Chris advises that the current delivery model works over the expected 20-year lifetime of the solar panels because of the subsidies that are offered by the UK government to those installing renewable energy. The 'feed-in tariff' (which is index-linked) offers a set amount for each unit (kilowatt hour or kWh) of electricity generated which is paid to the scheme by their chosen energy supplier. The government website notes that the rates of this 'generation tariff' vary depending on a number of factors:

- The size of your system

- What technology you install

- When your system was installed

- How energy efficient your home is

(Continued)

(Continued)

This is in addition to actually selling up to half the kilowatt hours back to the same energy supplier ('export tariff'), and whatever electricity is sold to the owners of the buildings hosting the solar panels. These government-set rates have changed since the Swansea scheme was established, so anyone wanting to set up a similar scheme in their area will need to develop their own financial model and potentially explore alternative delivery models to be sure it will be effective in terms of the efficiency of the solar technology they are proposing to use.

In Swansea, the technical and financial research had been done, and community engagement carried out to involved local people in SCEES, the new community benefit society. In the summer of 2016 SCEES were successful in securing a bridging loan to fund the capital installation of their first scheme. They worked with Robert Owen Community Banking, who were instrumental in ensuring the project was delivered, by providing a construction loan to finance the project.

Installing photovoltaic panels in a school in Swansea

After securing money to finance the installations, SCEES installed the specified solar panels on the roofs of nine schools and one residential care home owned by the City and County of Swansea. These buildings are situated in and around the wards of Townhill and Penderry – some of Wales's most deprived areas, which were deliberately targeted as they offered the greatest opportunity to make an impact in an area where this type of enterprise was not already happening.

SCEES entered into a 20-year lease and power purchase agreement with the building landlord and tenant in each case, enabling installation and maintenance of panels and the sale of some of the electricity generated on site to the tenant. Installations began at the start of the 2016 school summer holiday period and were completed by the end of September. Each installation will result in a cheaper, cleaner renewable source of energy for schools and a valuable educational resource as pupils will be able to interface with monitoring software and interpretation panels.

As a community benefit society, SCEES have been able to lock in a higher rate of Feed-in Tariff and so can provide a better financial return to schools, the community and also to investors. In terms of the sale of electricity between SCEES and the buildings' tenants (i.e. the schools), this is set out in a long-term Power Purchase Agreement between SCEES and the council with the rate set at half-way between the export tariff and the retail price of electricity. This will be reviewed on an annual basis.

SCEES ran a community share offer before Christmas 2016 aiming to raise £425,000 to pay off the short-term construction loan from Robert Owen Community Banking. Interested people were invited to become members of SCEES by investing in the scheme, and investors were offered a projected 6% annual rate of interest, with most of the surplus profits from future energy generation going into a community benefit fund. The money was raised inside seven weeks, with 200 new SCEES members paying £50 or more, two-thirds of whom were Swansea-based.

Chris notes that for such a community energy scheme to succeed, it is necessary to be able to take a long-term view. This is not usually a problem when talking to schools, but it is much more complex when trying to install on a number of domestic properties.

Meanwhile, the existing scheme is expected to raise over £500,000 during its 20-year lifetime from surplus profits once all incomings (subsidies and electricity payments) and outgoings (financing repayments, share interest and operational costs) have been taken into account. As dictated by the rules of the community benefit society, the amounts to be allocated locally from the resulting community fund have to be approved by the members at each annual general meeting. There is an interest in supporting the growth of renewable energy and enterprise development in the local community, but this may be subject to change depending on the needs of the community in the future.

Further Reading

Elias, Norbert (1939) *The Civilizing Process, Vols I and II*. Oxford: Blackwell, 1960 and 1982 (English translation from the German) – if you want to find out more about the idea of linking civilisation to self-restraint.

Schumacher, E.F. (1973) *Small is Beautiful*. London: Blond & Briggs – from an early stage of the environmental debate, but ranging more widely. You may find it says more than you remember.

Hopkins, Rob (2008) *The Transition Handbook - From Oil Dependency to Local Resilience*. Totnes: Green Books - I refer to this book several times in this work - you should read it, compare it to other approaches and information, and review your regeneration plans accordingly. The Handbook also has great practical guidance on local capacity building.

Mackay, David (2008) *Sustainable Energy - Without the Hot Air*. Cambridge: UIT Cambridge - a useful summary - downloadable from http://withouthotair.com/download.html (Accessed 14 June 2017).

For a range of publications about highways and transport, see the website for the Chartered Institution of Highways & Transportation at www.ciht.org.uk.

5

Sustainable Development I: Social Regeneration

Working with Your Local Community

From what we've said so far, I might have put this as the first chapter. This is the first of three chapters looking in more detail at the three-legged stool of sustainable development.

Community

What does 'community' mean to you?

- Fluffy – unfocused – wish list – impractical – and basically somebody else's worry (a trickle-down regeneration or bricks-and-mortar regeneration view)

- Anything not covered by economic development, land use planning or climate change (an academic view)

- Community is the only real issue, ignored by the *really* hard-to-reach groups – local government officers, outside experts and developers (a neighbourhood activist view)

The fact is, regeneration is a change process for the benefit of local people (including local businesses – 'the business community'), and if you're not doing it for the community, then you're doing it wrong. It's also enlightened self-interest to involve the community in regeneration, as they hold the key to resources not available to anyone else, know more about their local area, and the end result will be more long-lasting or 'sustainable' as a result.

'Community' of course is a broad term, and includes 'communities of place' (residents of a local area, who may not have much in common with each other) and 'communities of interest' (people who have things in common like sport and other cultural activities but don't necessarily live in the same street). Involving the community takes time, not least due to this diversity, but the different ways of doing so are well known (see Community Involvement later in the chapter), and more are being developed, such as through the 'Transition' movement. See also the lexicon of 'community' terms in Appendix 3, there's yards of them!

Anything without a community focus that looks like regeneration is more likely to be development, i.e. for private or corporate benefit. Development does of course bring some community benefits – some jobs for local people and more customers for local businesses, some physical improvements to derelict areas, and a general rise in local morale – and you will find significant people who think this is enough. However, the 'trickle-down' effect from development needs extra help through regulation and training to benefit local people, it doesn't happen on its own – particularly in so-called 'deprived' areas where morale is low – and doesn't happen at all if the jobs and trade (and houses) all go to outsiders.

Part of the regeneration programme for Gloucester included a redevelopment of derelict dock warehouses as a massive designer outlet centre called Gloucester Quays, but the development used no local firms, the main flooring came from China, no local city centre retailers took up premises (a condition of the planning permission), and when it was announced that 1,000 jobs had been created, only 36 were found to have gone to residents of the most deprived area in the county just nearby.

Subsequently, the focus on a walkway to encourage shoppers to walk the good half mile between the Quays and the city centre soaked up £7 million at the expense of £3 million slated for a self-sustaining neighbourhood centre with job training outputs for the most deprived wards in the county (see more detail in the case study in Chapter 3). And as a final twist, some of the new retail premises were later demolished to make way for other development without ever being occupied.

This is not to say that in physical terms the run-down dock areas don't look substantially better than before! And to be fair, there was going to be more regeneration between the city centre and the docks that became victim to government austerity cuts, and the original Regeneration Framework is still very much part of the City Council's agenda, but when the city centre areas remain in the 10 worst deprived areas for the county it's hard to be sure that the community has benefited as much as it might have done.

So let's go for more. The top prize for full, integrated and sustainable regeneration has yet to be won by anywhere in the UK – and possibly nowhere else either.

Sustainable Communities

The UK government defined 'sustainable communities' in 2005 as 'Places where people want to live and work, now and in the future'. They are:

1. **Active, inclusive and safe** – fair, tolerant and cohesive with a strong local culture and other shared community activities

2. **Well-run** – with effective and inclusive participation, representation and leadership

3. **Environmentally sensitive** – providing places for people to live that are considerate of the environment

4. **Well designed and built** – featuring a quality built and natural environment

5. **Well connected** – with good transport services and communication linking people to jobs, schools, health and other services

6. **Thriving** – with a flourishing and diverse local economy

7. **Well served** – with public, private, community and voluntary services that are appropriate to people's needs and accessible to all

8. **Fair for everyone** – including those in other communities, now and in the future

(HM Government, 2005: 74–6)

Official language, but you get the gist.

Quite a tall order, and pretty comprehensive – maybe this is why the perfectly regenerated place is yet to be seen!

How to achieve all the above? Well, that's the job, in your own time, starting from now. And in other people's time too, as this is clearly not a one-person task, is it? And while the order of priorities, detailed objectives and manner of achieving them will be different in every place, your solutions will be as good as anyone's, so please share your experiences with the rest of us so we learn from each other.

Meanwhile this definition still begs quite a few questions. How does it compare with your own world view or the views of local people where you are? Let's not be too complacent or blinkered but keep a perspective on what we're about.

Community Involvement

Quite often, the people wanting to start local regeneration schemes are newly arrived in the area – they've chosen it as a place to live, and now they want to make it better.

Fair enough, but such people really need to involve longer-term residents as well, not least because old-timers will know more about the place, and also because projects may suffer from lack of support if they're seen as solely for incomers.

There are many ways to start local conversations, for example:

- A household survey, particularly useful when developing parish plans – but check whether there have been other surveys first, or you may come up against 'consultation fatigue'

- A special family event with a board showing some local history and concerns, staffed by volunteers with clipboards who invite people to add their own views by using post-it notes – I've seen a variation on this theme using clothes pegs and a whirligig clothesline, and there'll be many others

- A series of public meetings with special topic speakers, followed by discussion and the sharing of ideas (I'm an old flipchart man myself)

These sessions must always be open to everyone, as must any working groups or actions that come out of them – always keep people genuinely involved and informed.

Community Empowerment

It's been said that nobody gives you power, you have to take it.

Money – land ownership – knowledge – electoral success – social standing – all these can bring power. Short of the revolution, however, the first step towards having some power over local regeneration is getting your presence known and your views heard.

In community terms this is often called 'giving people a voice', and is an important part of local 'capacity building' so that people can have their say in local regeneration.

Part of this is procedural:

1. Identify the different groups in your community

2. Visit them as the regeneration worker to make your face known and to understand their concerns and aspirations

3. Discuss whether they have common ground with other groups, or only issues particular to them

4. Decide with them whether they want their own 'voice', or whether they should join forces with others for greater impact

5. Set up with them a properly constituted and democratic basis for this 'voice' or voices – either as part of an existing power base or group or separately, but preferably involving some people in the process who already have power, such as local politicians (a vital connection, whether or not you personally agree with all their policies!)

6. Jointly debate and agree what the 'voice' is going to say, and how to say it to whom – newspapers have their own agenda, but harness the power of the media where you can

7. Support the early steps with publicity, minute-taking, etc., but always with the objective of people running their own show

Another part of empowerment is finding individuals who will stand up in public and lend their vocal chords to the cause. 'Champions' is a good name for these, but be careful to set out the democratic ground rules before you start, or you may find you have empowered strong people with loud voices who end up only talking about their personal concerns, and the silent majority are left behind once more ...

Thirdly, knowledge is the key to this kind of power:

• Knowledge of what is happening with all the players

• Knowledge of what local people think about that

• Knowledge of when, where and how to put your oar in

Empowerment only works if you end up getting – and keeping – a seat where the decisions are being made and one from which you can speak and influence the decisions.

Campaigning

Sometimes, despite all your efforts to gain a local consensus of what is best for your local area, someone else imposes something which clearly will not be helpful and which you feel you must simply join others in the community in opposing.

> The French as a nation seem particularly good at rallying against local idiocies, and it can be done in the UK as well – witness the successful campaign in the picturesque town of Hay-on-Wye to prevent the imposition of a new and unwanted supermarket.

There are books on this of course, though beware of inveterate campaigners on the ground who may not be from your area and who love standing up against things but aren't always clear in what they say or controllable in what they do.

The main thing I would recommend if a campaign is unavoidable is to go hard from the outset. Get your facts straight, gather local feelings and rally support, and then go for the jugular at once, and keep at it. This is absolutely necessary if the people who have made the misguided decision are equally adamant they are in the right, and if it is a local government decision there may be procedural opportunities to challenge it that disappear if too much time is allowed to pass.

And whether or not you and the local community are successful in reversing the decision, at the very least people will think twice about not consulting everyone properly in the future! But be controlled in your actions, don't throw away the credibility that is necessary for the other things you have to do. Confrontation and regeneration make bad bedfellows, so go for consensus wherever possible.

One of the things I say to people who start on a campaign is – what if you win? It's important (and it also boosts a positive outlook among your supporters and partners) to plan the next steps should your approach succeed and you gain your objective.

Of course, you may not get everything you want all at once, particularly if the matter is complex. If you are looking ahead to managing a community asset or service, such as (in my own experience) a community-run library, in between campaigning and managing there will probably be some negotiation. When bridging the gap, be clear about your maximum and minimum positions – what you are campaigning for, and the minimum position you and the community would be prepared to accept – before sitting down with the other side.

Different strokes for different folks – however it all turns out, you will probably find some people who were campaigners slipping away, and some others coming forward to help with the managing. Expect a change of guard from campaigners to volunteers once you have achieved your objective.

Community Cohesion

Communities can be pretty diverse, particularly in urban areas. There will need to be some appreciation of each other and some coming together to produce a full community approach to regeneration.

> For example, we know that Moslems pray towards Mecca five times a day, but that means in daylight. In the UK in November, recommended prayer times in the afternoon are 1 p.m., 3 p.m. and 4 p.m., so city centres without prayer facilities will be less friendly for Moslem visitors, shoppers or workers. (Interestingly, friends from Holland say they expect to see town centre mosques.)

This leads us into the differences between people of different cultures. If there are only two such groups in a community, the differences are stark and there is always the danger of conflict. This suggests to me that places where there is a multi-layered society have an important role in showing how different groups can live together in practice.

The 'multi-cultural' melting pot idea sounds fine in theory, but doesn't respect different people's beliefs. Most religions teach that faith is a gift from God, but some people find it hard to believe that applies to other people's faiths as well, and lest we forget, there are also people who think this life is all there is – they too need their community's care.

Perhaps we can agree to appreciate our own culture while respecting other people's differences, but that's only a starting position – how about living to please our neighbours as well as ourselves? We can measure success simply by people being able to say 'hello' to each other in the street.

Religion is only one issue of course. There can be communal differences around age, race, cultural heritage, disability – in fact everything that distinguishes one person from another. Each issue has its fine points and its support groups, and all are subject to prejudice of different kinds.

Of course, if community cohesion was easy, everyone would be doing it already – sounds like a valid issue for a regeneration worker.

Community Structures

In the early days of writing this book, I was asked what I was going to include about minorities. This puzzled me at first, because I firmly believe in involving the whole community in regeneration anyway, but it got me thinking about how we sustain community efforts in the longer term.

The same regeneration worker won't always necessarily be there (and would be worn out if so!), and the same would apply to key people getting together on a regeneration steering group. In the same way as building build-ings for the long term requires proper planning, creating the right community structures to maintain longer-term action is also very important – and impor-tant that they are inclusive of the whole community, not exclusive to one social group.

In some places there will be existing and constitutionally robust organisa-tions like local parish councils, which I talk about in the next section. In others, there will be a need to create something new, but fortunately (in the UK at least) there are several models to choose from.

The first question of course is why – why are you thinking you might need a new structure or organisation? Thinking about aims and objectives – what you are collectively seeking to achieve – will help you to choose from the 20 or so options available.

There are a number of points you can cover, including:

- Will it need a long life?

- Will it need to raise money, which implies a bank account?

- Will it need to own property?

- Will it need to get rents from a building, or to trade?

- Will it need to pay staff, which implies a formal structure?

- Will it benefit from having open community membership?

- Will it benefit from fixed links to some existing organisations or groups?

The simplest structure has been called an 'unincorporated voluntary body', which is just a number of people getting together for a one-off project, such as a campaign or an environmental clean-up, after which they can disband. There might be an agreement on how you will manage your meetings and activities – 'terms of reference' – also listing who is in the group, but that's all.

Some of the most common constitutional options for longer-term purposes:

- **Company limited by guarantee** – has been the most commonly used option, with a similar structure to many commercial companies, but often com-bined with charitable status. Beginning to be replaced by

- **Charitable incorporated organisation** – similar to a company format, but with built-in charitable status so only one set of financial reports is needed each year (as opposed to one to Companies House and one to the Charity Commission)

- **Community interest company** – has an 'asset lock' to help secure from future sale assets such as buildings used for community purposes

- **Community benefit society** – commonly called a cooperative, a succes-sor since 2014 to the old industrial and provident societies which were membership-owned organisations with a slightly freer hand when it came to trading. Charitable status is gained from HM Revenue & Customs via the Financial Conduct Authority rather than from the Charity Commission

Charitable status is useful for two reasons:

- It encourages people to give it donations and grants – and for some funders, charitable status is a requirement

- It allows for relief from local taxes such as business rates, though only for premises solely used for charitable purposes

Contrary to popular belief, it does *not* give you freedom from value-added tax (VAT) or other UK government taxes!

There used to be four charitable objects that supported charitable status. Now there are 13, but since March 1999 regeneration has been given its own wording, which could usefully be embedded in whole or in part within whichever constitution is chosen:

> The promotion for the benefit of the public of urban or rural regeneration in areas of social and economic deprivation (and in particular in [specify area]) by all or any of the following means:
>
> a. the relief of financial hardship;
>
> b. the relief of unemployment;
>
> c. the advancement of education, training or retraining, particularly among unemployed people, and providing unemployed people with work experience;
>
> d. the provision of financial assistance, technical assistance or business advice or consultancy in order to provide training and employment opportunities for unemployed people in cases of financial or other charitable need through help;
>
>> i.   in setting up their own business, or
>>
>> ii. to existing businesses;
>
> e. the creation of training and employment opportunities by the provision of workspace, buildings, and/or land for use on favourable terms;
>
> f. the provision of housing for those who are in conditions of need and the improvement of housing in the public sector or in charitable ownership provided that such power shall not extend to relieving any local authorities or other bodies of a statutory duty to provide or improve housing;
>
> g. the maintenance, improvement or provision of public amenities;
>
> h. the preservation of buildings or sites of historic or architectural importance;

i.   the provision of recreational facilities for the public at large or those who by reason of their youth, age, infirmity or disablement, financial hardship or social and economic circumstances, have need of such facilities;

j.   the protection or conservation of the environment;

k.   the provision of public health facilities and childcare;

l.   the promotion of public safety and prevention of crime;

m.   such other means as may from time to time be determined subject to the prior written consent of the Charity Commissioners for England and Wales.

(Review of the Register Report, 1999: 3)

A pretty broad but familiar-sounding list!

There are extra obligations on a charity, which you will need to investigate before making your final choice of structure:

- Any financial surpluses must be used for community not private benefit

- Directors or trustees cannot usually be salaried or paid

- Trading in goods other than those connected to your 'primary purpose' (for example a community library could sell reading glasses) is limited to a percentage of your turnover (a community library has no clear connection to selling overseas holidays!)

There are even some computer programs that will lead you through the various options – get some advice on the best structure for you.

One of the key questions when setting up a new organisation is how many trustees or directors there will be.

Getting back to the question of minorities, it is very important that whatever you do in regeneration, you double-check how it may impact on people with different health and lifestyle issues and from different cultural backgrounds before you go ahead. This is not the same as having every minority group represented on your board!

Gloucester City Council used to have two special interest forums that met regularly, one for people with disabilities and one for racial equality, which provided a sounding board for all aspects of the council's work, and minority groups were invited to attend. The chairs of each group were then the obvious people to contact about any new initiative, but that was for an overall population of 120,000 people and may not be appropriate in your area.

We don't want tokenism of course, we want results that take every-one into consideration. It is certainly dangerous to have a board or steering group made up of all the same kind of people who may then be swayed collectively by certain points of view and not take a sufficiently broad approach (I think of the 'men in suits' nature of at least one regeneration board of my experience). But trying to get every viewpoint in the room for every meeting will be a self-defeating exercise.

Above all, we want a size and make-up of group that can work effectively together, and is properly chaired. So often we find that newcomers to an area are the ones taking a lead in improvements for the future – fine, but make sure some long-term residents are involved as well, as they have local experience and networks to offer. People who are difficult to deal with may be better as regular consultees rather than core decision-makers, and characters that are too over-bearing – from whatever background – may also produce a skewed result. Representatives from local councils are important to consider because of their connections, but not too many, and no more than one from each council!

In summary, try to think of everyone in the community and all the ramifications when planning your proposals – but don't have an unwieldy structure to implement them, make it straightforward to go ahead as a working group and make a difference. I would say there would have to be a very good reason for having more than six to twelve people on your board.

Local Councils

In the UK, the area around an established Christian church is called its parish.

In most parts of the country, the parish became a useful basis for civil administration, with its own parish council structures but not necessarily tied to the same geographic boundaries as the ecclesiastical parish.

There are no such civil parishes in Northern Ireland. There are community councils in Scotland but without any statutory powers, and they operate principally as links between district-level authorities and the local community. In Wales there are community councils with some statutory powers, and in England parish councils remain as the lowest or first tier of local government. There are over 9,000 of them in England, though some city areas no longer have them. The advantages of a parish council include:

- Their high profile with the local community

- Their formal links with other local government bodies

- Their wide scope for action

- Their ability to raise local taxes ('the parish precept') in order to fund their activities, including paying for staff

- Their ability to borrow capital sums from the Public Works Loan Board, repayable from local taxes

The interesting news is that if you don't have a parish or community council in your area, the government allows you to create one. This has most famously been done in Queen's Park, the first area in London to have a parish/community council in many years. It came into being following the election of 12 councillors in May 2014, and in its first year raised £136,897 from its 12,500 residents (roughly £11 per head). So if you're in an area of England or Wales that doesn't have a parish or community council but this model sounds attractive, look into it!

In terms of scope for action, UK legislation determines what a parish council may spend its money on. Much (but not all) of this power comes from the Local Government Act 1972, and overall it includes:

- The acquisition of buildings and land

- Community bus services

- Community centres and village halls

- Footpath repair and maintenance

- Parish events

- Public parks and toilets

- Trade fairs and more

And under certain circumstances ('the power of competence') parish councils can undertake anything an individual might do, so there is broad scope for regeneration activities. More details on statutory powers in England and Wales are available from *Arnold-Baker on Local Council Administration* (see Clayden, 2016), but here is a taster selection of the range of projects recently reported by parish and town councils in England, and there are many more examples across the UK:

- Devolution of local services – markets, parks and open spaces, playgrounds, toilets (Newark Town Council, Nottinghamshire)

- Havercroft Community Library (Havercroft with Cold Hiendley Parish Council, West Yorkshire)

- Helston and The Lizard Works – local employment project (Helston Town Council, Cornwall)

- Self-Build Housing (Frome Town Council, Somerset)

- TACTIC – Teenage Advice Centre/Teenage Information Centre (Leighton-Linslade Town Council, Bedfordshire)

Culture

I used to think culture was about opera and fine art. UNESCO defines culture differently:

> the set of distinctive spiritual, material, intellectual and emotional features of society or a social group, that encompasses, in addition to art and literature, lifestyles, ways of living together, value systems, traditions and beliefs.
>
> (UNESCO, 2001: 4)

This definition can be broken down into seven main headings:

1. Ethnic identity and belief

2. Heritage and the arts

3. Learning

4. Parks and open space

5. Buildings

6. Sport

7. Leisure and tourism

This approach sits very well with someone who thinks joined-up regeneration is the way to go! Food and drink and clothing need to fit in there somewhere as well.

Culture is about people, really, and the things that reflect a group of people, and this definition provides another helpful checklist of things to cover in regeneration. One common application is the 'Percent for Art' – 1% of the value of any major development work to be spent on aspects of 'public art', anything from individual artworks (local artists?) to things like floor mosaics with local designs, but all reflecting aspects of the local community. There is a view that culture should be a fourth leg of sustainable development, a vital part of communities taking charge of their own futures, and this idea is underpinned by the importance given to Welsh culture in the Wellbeing of Future Generations (Wales) Act 2015.

How's the world view coming along, by the way?

Case Study: Incredible Edible Todmorden

You may have heard about this as a novel project that makes use of a wide range of small patches of urban ground to grow fruit and vegetables for the local community to pick freely – but it's much more than that.

(Continued)

(Continued)

Todmorden is a market town on the Lancashire/Yorkshire border in northern England. The story began when local resident Pam Warhurst heard Professor Tim Lang speak at a conference on climate change in 2007. He challenged the audience to start growing more food – for the sake of the planet.

Pam began to wonder if it was possible to take a town like Todmorden and, just by focusing on local food, start creating the shifts in behaviour we need to live within the resources we have. Everyone understands food – could growing food be the catalyst for people to start taking responsibility for their own futures?

Pam talked it over with her friend Mary Clear, and Mary began to plant vegetables in her front garden, with a sign: 'Help Yourselves'. It got people talking. Other people rallied to the cause. Mysteriously, herbs and vegetables started sprouting on other sites in the town. That started a few more conversations. With trepidation they organised their first public meeting. More than 60 people came and the air was electric. They knew they were on to something. Some of them started volunteering, clearing waste ground, building raised beds and, always, planting more veg.

The Incredible Edible Todmorden challenge was underway. A challenge with three underpinning principles:

- Action not words

- We are not victims

- Stop passing the buck

This wasn't just about self sufficiency. What is now being achieved is far bigger. Through the shared language of food, the people of a small town are engaging in the biggest challenge facing the human race as they put it: how to ensure a secure future for the planet. Through action, everyone has started to understand a bit more about the world around them. With this understanding has come a greater sense of responsibility, and through that it has become clear that things have to be done differently – and that everyone has to be involved.

The Todmorden model can be thought of as three spinning plates:

- The Community Plate – growing produce and working together

- The Learning Plate – providing training from field to classroom to kitchen

- The Business Plate – supporting local commerce

Spinning any one of these can bring real benefits, but spinning all three together gives a simple and engaging plan of action for a stronger town. There are no paid staff, everyone is a volunteer – and people are encouraged to join in by a simple headline:

If You Eat – You Are In!

You can find out more from the project website, but current activities include:

- Some 60 tours every year for over 1,000 visitors (who shop in the town)
- Cookery demonstrations and free tastings
- Free Harvest Festival
- Free talks and workshops
- Kidsfest, a day-long creative activity day for kids
- Lending tents and flags and cooking kit to other local groups
- The Todmorden Incredible Foodie Fortnight.

There have also been two spin-off ventures, learning centres at the Incredible Aqua Garden and the Incredible Farm.

In 2012, the Incredible Edible Network was set up in response to the huge popularity of the original group in Todmorden and the flood of enquiries from those who wanted to embrace its aims. With the help of a three-year grant-funded Network Facilitator, the number of Incredible Edible groups in the UK has soared from 25 to more than 100, and the movement is hugely popular across the globe. Facebook fans are now in their thousands, and conferences and workshops are held across the country. The Network looks to promote sustainable food production and consumption in local and national policy, practice and decision-making.

And the final amazing thing – the keynote for this movement is Kindness – a word that is actually posted up without further explanation all around Todmorden.

Kindness is key

(Continued)

(Continued)

As the current chair Mary Clear explains:

> We can send a man to Mars, but a third of the world have no ready access to water or toilet facilities. Money or politics won't solve this. Kindness is the only way to improvement – if each person is trying to be a bit kinder to each other, then we can make a real difference.

Further Reading

Proctor, Keith (ed.) (2001) *Community-Led Regeneration Handbook*. Totnes: Churches National Housing Coalition (UK) – a summary of good practice produced by residents for residents, featuring five success stories of estate regeneration in Plymouth, London, Liverpool, Walsall and Bradford.

The National Association of Local Councils (NALC) publish some guidance on setting up parish councils under the banner 'Power to the People'! The guidance comes in two parts – Section 1 is What Are Local Councils? and Section 2 is How To Create Your Own Local Council – both downloadable at www.nalc.gov.uk/publications (Accessed 14th June 2017).

6

Sustainable Development II: Economic Regeneration

Local and Global Economies

'The market will solve everything', 'The market always rights itself' – well, we've seen occasions in the early 21st century where the global market has got itself into fast-running waters and has needed public money to bail it out. And if it *had* been left to 'right itself', there would have been a lot of human loss in the process. Let's be sure we're basing our grandchildren's futures on as sound a basis as possible.

Economic Theory

I wish I could have found the quote about all economists being right, except they say all the others are wrong, but these will have to do:

> The First Law of Economists: For every economist, there exists an equal and opposite economist.
>
> The Second Law of Economists: They're both wrong. (David Wildasin)
>
> Give me a one-handed economist. All my economists say, on the one hand … on the other … (Harry S. Truman, US president, 1945–53)
>
> Economics is the only field in which two people can get a Nobel Prize for saying exactly the opposite thing. (Anon.)

I'm pretty sure economic purists of whatever persuasion will be unhappy about the perspective that follows, but I've been trying to find a way for ordinary local people to grapple with unfamiliar ideas about the economy and jobs, so they can begin to make some decisions.

Mickey Marx Economics

Do you know the difference between a sink, a bath and a hoover?

- Sink – something that absorbs money and does nothing with it
- Bath – something that keeps money in circulation in the local economy
- Hoover – something that sucks money out of the local economy

These are terms from an attempt in the 1980s to provide a science to distinguish between local and global economies (I wish I'd noted the names of the people leading the seminar I attended), dubbed 'Mickey Marx Economics' by an unfriendly critic who thought it too simplistic.

The 'global economy' is something we've become used to – imports from around the world (do we really need tropical fruit everywhere – what is the real cost including wastage?), factories relocating from industrialised nations to countries where the cost of living is much lower, supermarkets replacing local shops, buying via the Internet.

Every place that has lost or gained jobs and prosperity due to the global economy will have a story to tell. On the other hand, with international financial markets being so powerful (25% of the UK economy is based in the City of London, for example), how do we make local decisions about economic regeneration?

We need some kind of picture of the local economy. Every area will produce some of the necessities of life – food, water, shelter, clothing, domestic supplies, business supplies, fuel and power – but probably not all, so local barter is probably not the whole answer, we need to make money to buy in what we don't produce. Not everywhere can sell something to China (any Chinese goods in your house?), but if there are 'hoovers' taking money from your area (and there will be), what about 'hoovers' of our own that bring in cash from outside?

Some people will commute to work outside your area (and hoover money in), and some like me will work at home and then someone from outside sends a cheque (all being well!). If we can make things from (preferably renewable) local materials to sell elsewhere, that's a great hoover. Making things for outside firms that have local factories is not so profitable, but at least you're sharing in their global success.

A common economic concern is where local manufacturing or mining has failed, leaving many local people without an income – this tends to leave derelict industrial sites too, which become a prime focus for regeneration. A related question is, must people move to find work, or could they re-train and learn to make money some other way? Simply bringing in a big supermarket to re-sell us the necessities of life (and hoover the profits elsewhere) is not a long-term answer.

I'm told one supermarket chain set up a sandwich-making factory in an ex-mining area in Derbyshire to provide local work. Hmmm. Haven't tracked this story down yet.

About this time in the debate someone will come forward with some economic proposals for your area, and this is where you as the regeneration worker come in.

Firstly, let's be sure anyone making economic proposals has clearly done their homework. 'Economic assessment' is becoming a familiar discipline, but it's all too easy for consultants to present the same wisdom they have presented in other places. For example, it has been a common saying in the UK for many years that manufacturing is dying, but in Cinderford in 1996 manufacturing of all kinds was 50% of the local economy, and much of it is still there – so let's observe trends by all means, but without by thought or deed hastening the end of businesses we already have, as that would be a real own goal.

Secondly, sustainability – are existing or future enterprises going to provide long-term economic stability for local people? If something only has a projected life of 20 years, let's know about it if we can. Simply giving people more choice (such as new shopping malls pandering to 'consumerism') is not a long-term boon if other ventures are going to go bust as a result – and anything solely dependent on the global economy is as vulnerable as anything solely local (can the global economy survive without the motor car?), so let's not blindly do what other places are doing, it may not work here.

Thirdly, local benefit – if we accept that wealth is a better aim than poverty, how do we support local prosperity? Just focusing on 'baths' – locally-owned businesses – is not the whole story, as there can clearly be some local benefits from the global economy, such as if a local factory produces something in global demand. This is where we should be asking close questions about whether new ventures take more out of the local economy than they put in. And economic assessments are only useful if they're written in words that everyone can understand.

Funnily enough, the need to think about local people is even clearer when you have too much wealth moving in. It's a fact in much of rural England for example – especially within commuting distance of the City of London – that expensive incomers drive up the price of houses so that local residents can't afford them. A friend of mine has called this 'ethnic cleansing by money', and it ain't regeneration – let's find ways such as taxing second homes or selling expensive goods to hoover money in these situations to support local people.

If climate change and financial markets continue to gang up on us, then we'll really be looking at how local people can be self-sufficient in the necessities of life.

Mickey Marx perhaps, but if we accept the need for a local 'balance of payments' (and I haven't even mentioned taxes or investments), let's try to assess the local economy on its own merits rather than making impulsive decisions, because new jobs and shops may hide a darker underlying trend. And don't try to freeze-frame the economy either – it's a living thing (therefore difficult to pin down), so never assume you've got the final answer.

This approach suggests there should be some effective balance between the local and the global economy in each area, but there is another approach being taken by the 'Transition initiatives', which is that a more exciting, inclusive and ultimately safer approach is to work towards a much more localised economy anyway. This means challenging what Rob Hopkins calls the myths that underpin modern UK culture:

> that the future will be wealthier than the present, that economic growth can continue indefinitely, that we have become such an individualistic society that any common goals are unthinkable, that possessions can make you happy, and that economic globalisation is an inevitable process to which we have all given our consent.
>
> (Hopkins, 2008: 14)

One summary of the 'localisation' approach is given in the Energy Descent Action Plan for Totnes in Devon:

> This Plan explores the nuts-and-bolts practicalities of relocalising the economy of the area. It argues that in a world of highly volatile oil prices, the need for stringent cuts in carbon emissions and economic uncertainty, the globalised economy upon which we are so dependent can no longer be relied upon, indeed it leaves us highly vulnerable. At the moment, Totnes and its surrounding parishes act like a large leaky bucket. Money pours into the area through wages, grants, pensions, funding, tourist revenues and so on. In our current economic model, most of it pours back out again, and its ability to make things happen locally is lost. Each time we pay our energy bill, that money leaves the area. Each time we shop in a supermarket, 80% of that money leaves the area. Every time we shop online, that money that could have bolstered our economy leaves the area. All the while, pressure grows on our local shops and businesses.
>
> At the same time, local agriculture employs fewer and fewer people each year, more and more food is imported, new buildings are created from materials from around the world, and most of the goods sold in the shops of Totnes have travelled long distances to get there. The concept of localisation is about shifting the focus of production closer to home. It is not something that can be done overnight, it is a long-term process that requires planning, design and innovation.
>
> (Hodgson with Hopkins, 2010: 18)

Time to check your world view again – I'm checking mine.

Business

Businesses and business people are not all the same. Large businesses in particular are not full of entrepreneurs, and there is a world of difference between the different spheres of manufacturing, distribution (including retail), and the many service and specialised industries from banking to healthcare to sport.

Each type of business will need its own conditions in order to thrive, and while these can be studied in depth, there are a few questions to ask when considering local regeneration:

* What is the particular value of your location to business?

* What can outside firms bring in, such as new financing, or filling service gaps in local business areas ('supply chains'), that cannot be provided by locally-owned businesses that reinvest their profits locally?

* What then is the balance between encouraging new businesses and supporting the ones you already have?

There is a strong temptation to improve local areas with new buildings and worry about the health of the businesses that inhabit them later. Sustainability is also about economic prosperity, so do your research first.

And get to know your local businesses, it will repay you a thousand-fold – they're run by people who work with people, after all, go out and meet them.

Entrepreneurship

Developing local firms is a valid objective for a regeneration programme, particularly encouraging and supporting local start-ups. What kind of business is going to be successful in your area? If we all knew what was going to make money, we'd all be doing it!

There are many types and industries to choose from, including:

- Communications
- Distribution
- Finance
- Hospitality
- Import/export
- Manufacturing
- Retail
- Services

Entrepreneurship is about the right person having the right idea at the right time and in the right place, and seeing it through.

If they've not been in business before, budding entrepreneurs will be glad of all kinds of support and advice, particularly financial (what accounting systems do I need, what about tax?) and legal (do I have to be a limited company, what about employing staff?). As most will be starting off as sole traders, relying on their own efforts, one of the best things to suggest is that they answer these questions about themselves:

- Why are you interested in starting your own business?
- How much time and energy do you have?
- What are your specific objectives relating to earnings/family/life?
- What aims do you have for this business?
- What in, a single phrase, is your business idea?
- What is your Unique Selling Proposition (USP)?
- Who needs your product or service?
- Who are you competing against?

Statistics show a high percentage of start-up businesses fail in the first two years – it's worth some effort to keep that figure down in your regeneration area, so make sure suitable business advice is available – and free for the first conversation.

Social Enterprise

These are businesses that don't return profits to their directors or owners, but are community-owned ventures whose profits are either reinvested or otherwise used for public benefit. They are a growing feature of the UK regeneration scene, with government blessing, not least as with potentially fewer overheads they can deliver otherwise costly public services, and take on businesses like pubs and village shops that have failed financially.

'Business' is the key word, as while there may be particular local opportunities for social enterprise, they have to make a profit ('surplus') like any other business. You will need someone with an entrepreneurial approach to develop the business – that may sound obvious, but not everyone in the private sector for example has started a business, many will work in other people's firms.

> On the other hand, while those in the public or voluntary sector may have the right social ethos, they are not necessarily adept at running a social enterprise. One community project leader raised thousands for a new community building by focusing on local needs, but then didn't change focus and kept services going even when the costs of those services were dragging the bank account into the red.

So some key questions you should ask about a proposed social enterprise (as any other business) are:

- Who are the proposed customers, and what's their spending power? Do they want what you're offering?

- What is the competition that might take your customers?

- How long will this business opportunity last – are you going to be providing something that people will want (and pay for) for a long time? If it's a service contract, how secure is the contract?

- Can you afford this business – are the set-up or running costs going to exceed your income? (Failure to cover your running costs is the original sin of enterprise)

- Who is going to run the business – are they the right people, and are they getting the right advice?

There are a number of common constitutional models for social enterprises in the UK that control how they are governed (see also Community Structures in Chapter 5):

- **Companies limited by guarantee** – same as any other limited company, whereby if the directors act properly then their only liability in case of financial disaster is limited, usually, to £10. Registered at Companies House in the UK, where you can get model constitutions ('Memorandum and Articles of Association')

- **Community benefit societies** – linked to the old (though still vibrant) cooperative movement, where people club together for a particular purpose

- **Community interest companies** – a new model in the UK, available through the Internet, with a key feature of an 'asset lock' which prevents any properties the community run being sold off for private gain

You will need to choose the right model depending on where your income will come from. Some people assume becoming a charity is the way forward, but unless you are only collecting rents from a building, UK charitable status sets severe restrictions on how you can trade or otherwise make money. On the other hand, many national charities won't consider giving money to local ventures unless they *are* registered charities!

If charitable fundraising is vital, one way forward is this: have your building or any other assets that you make money from owned by a company registered as a charity, but run them through a subsidiary company (not a charity) that covenants its profits to the head charity. This provides the double benefit that if your trading arm goes bust, the asset stays in community ownership.

Whichever model is chosen, the vital element is the people – members of the community who can be truly enterprising (see Further Reading *The Social Entrepreneur*). Look for that real enthusiasm, dedication and open-mindedness.

Economic Development

This is about what you can do to encourage the local economy – not what local firms do, that's just business.

There are a number of possible activities, for example:

- Developing facilities for business advice and support

- Encouraging 'shop local' campaigns and local supply chains to keep money in the local economy

- Improving local marketing and signposting

- Supporting environmental, communications, transport and other infrastructure improvements

- Tendering public services to local firms (why can't all public authorities have the same clearly-labelled 'procurement' section on their websites?)

- Training local people for employment, or self-employment

It is not usually permissible to just give public money to private businesses, but one useful local government approach is giving 50% grants for painting shopfronts. This is acceptable because even if the public don't enter the shop they still benefit from the improved street scene. Add in paint sponsorship from a local firm, and even advice from local designers, and maybe a scheme for bulk buying of hanging baskets, and you have a really good start to a town regeneration scheme.

Not that this is going to revive your shopping streets and solve all your local economic worries at a stroke, but it's a good, visible 'quick win'. Incidentally, be careful about too much focus on empty shops – this is also a very visible issue to local people (and voters), but some turnover in shop use and occupation is inevitable, and empty shops are as much an indicator of other problems with the economy than a core problem in themselves. Filling the shops with businesses that take money out of the local economy may bring in some customers for the more long-standing businesses, but will not necessarily jump-start the local economy overall without bringing in some other economic development measures as well.

Training for Employment

One common objective of regeneration is more jobs for local people, but the systems to link people to new work are not always effective.

There are a number of elements that need to connect (and consequently several bodies that need to be involved):

- Creation of new jobs, either by incoming firms or from local expansion (economic development)

- New jobs made available to local people (planning policy, support of business organisations)

- Local people made aware of new jobs (range of mechanisms including job centres/labour exchanges)

- Local people trained to apply for and carry out new jobs (training organisations and initiatives of all kinds)

- Funding available to support all the above (public and private sector)

A ground-breaking approach was taken in 1994 by the London Borough of Greenwich, which set up a scheme in partnership with the local job centre (labour exchange) to ensure local people were employed in building the new Millennium Dome (now the O2 Centre). This was so effective that the initiative expanded, and 10 years later GLLAB (Greenwich Local Labour and Business) had a staff of 33 people, one of whom was permanently employed finding funding for the other 32!

Matching local people to work through training, the approach taken by GLLAB, needed to be backed up by firms offering work to local people in the first place. Greenwich Borough required all developers to attend to this as part of gaining planning permission, and something like this may need to be part of official planning policy if you wish to apply it in your area.

For the rest, linking job opportunities to local people through training can be achieved through good partnership working. Gloucester took a leaf out of Greenwich's book, researched the local labour market and training organisations, carried out a pilot scheme with local employers, and developed a fully-fledged 'Gloucester Works' scheme with multi-million government and European funding. So it may be daunting, but it can be done. And as there are so many organisations to be involved, you don't have to be an expert in all parts of the scheme in order to start the ball rolling, as no one else will be that expert either – in fact, you can start without being expert in any of them (as we did), just have that calm determination to achieve a result.

Apprenticeships

Starting young as a trainee in an established business has a very long tradition. One perception of medieval England is that when the town-based craft guilds got going, you needed to belong to a guild to have regular work – but crafts and guilds always needed new people too, and couldn't always get them from the obvious places, such as extended families or recommendations from patrons.

In the modern era, the underlying economic principle is still the same – there needs to be something in it for both (or all) parties. When times are tough, companies of all sizes make economies, whether in marketing, training, or other areas, and so governments have an opportunity to get involved in schemes to encourage firms to take on apprentices as part of a wider governmental approach to reducing unemployment and encouraging productivity, which benefits everyone (including the taxman, of course!).

The rationale for government intervention is further described in a July 2015 report for the Social Market Foundation by Professor Alison Wolf:

> Turning apprenticeship back into an institution which reflects labour market needs, develops young people's skills to a high level, and makes a genuine contribution to productivity, requires at least two major changes.
>
> First, it requires a major shift in the whole way the system is organized, and a return to the employer–apprentice contract as central and defining. Otherwise, the characteristics which make apprenticeship

valuable – close links with actual workplace activity and requirements, and sizeable investment of the employer's time and attention – will remain absent …

Second, and equally critical, apprenticeship needs more money. An apprenticeship system which is worth having will, on average, involve far higher spending per apprentice than under the dysfunctional and increasingly discredited one that recent UK governments constructed. We do not need tens of thousands more low-level apprentices in retail and business. We do need thousands more high-level ones in engineering, construction, and IT, all of which register acute skill shortages.

(Woolf, 2015: 12)

The background to this report was the proposal that the UK government establish an apprenticeship levy, whereby all firms pay 0.5% of their payroll bill into a national apprenticeship scheme – the vast majority of firms being protected from the economic effects of this by a £15,000 allowance. This new approach has since been confirmed from April 2017, when there is an expectation that some £3 billion will be raised every year to fund apprentice training.

The details of how this new scheme will work have been published by the UK government's Skills Funding Agency (2016). Of course, there have been a myriad of other approaches to apprenticeships, and even some parish councils have got involved, such as Painswick Parish Council in Gloucestershire. As the local regeneration worker interested in supporting the local economy, you will do well to spend some time researching the practicalities of apprenticeships in your local area, and encouraging local firms to use this approach to employ more local people.

Case Study: Forest of Dean Entrepreneurs

In the UK there used to be a government-funded support service for businesses including start-ups called 'Business Link'. I shared an office with the Cinderford branch in 1996, but when the government withdrew the service there was a gap that needed to be filled.

A pilot scheme for the Forest of Dean was developed under the auspices of Adult Education in Gloucestershire, with pump-prime funding from Jobcentre Plus (the government's labour exchange) and the Forest of Dean District Council. In October 2011, Miranda Jenkins, a self-employed training provider, won the tender to become programme facilitator, and then brought me in to join her due to my experience of working with the community and other local connections.

(Continued)

(Continued)

The 'Forest Business Incubator' pilot worked very well, with over 80 local people engaged of whom around 50 made steps towards developing their own business. Part of the pilot was about approaching larger local businesses to fund the continuation of the mentoring and training service, and this was also working well, but while Adult Education in Gloucestershire continued to provide funds towards training events, unfortunately the other pump-prime funding was no longer available from the end of March 2012.

Having provided a much-needed local service and raised local expectations, Miranda and I were keen to work with existing and potentially new partners to keep the project going. We held a series of stakeholder meetings, at which it was agreed that the surest foundation for the future was extended sponsorship from local businesses, rather than relying on grants from external bodies. There was also much discussion about the name of the project, and it was decided to rename it 'The Forest of Dean Entrepreneurs', looking ahead to a potential membership scheme.

We were successful in attracting 10 sponsors for a three-year programme with the help of Graham Wildin, an existing sponsor and local accountant. Some larger firms came forward because they wished to support the Forest generally, while others such as lawyers, accountants and printers had a further interest as providers of business services. The project was then relaunched in February 2013 with myself as project coordinator and Miranda leading in the training.

At our first event in March 2013 in Cinderford we had 19 people interested in starting up their own business! Numbers at start-up events have fluctuated since, partly reflecting the varying level of unemployment in the Forest, but we have also put on specialist courses to meet local demand, covering areas such as marketing (the most popular) and using social media for business, usually with invited speakers. We also started the Forest Enterprise Fair in November 2013 – to link with Global Entrepreneurship Week – and four years later this is established as the only regular business-to-business event in the Forest of Dean.

Over 400 people have now been engaged with information, training or other support since the relaunch in 2013. We have successfully renewed our sponsorship levels for another two years – some existing sponsors, some new – and started to reach out more to existing small businesses as well as start-ups through a series of evening 'Meet and Learn' events in local pubs. We are developing connections with the local branch of the Federation of Small Business and holding discussions with the Gloucestershire First Local Enterprise Partnership about closer links with the county 'Growth Hub' based in Gloucester.

We always said we wouldn't keep the project going willy-nilly, only if there was continued demand for its services. Miranda and I have been able to step back from the project – Miranda to further develop her training business, and me to write this book! – but we are enormously proud of what we and the project partners and volunteer steering group have achieved to date, and who knows what the future will bring?

The fourth Forest Enterprise Fair, 15 November 2016

Further Reading

Mawson, Andrew (2008) *The Social Entrepreneur*. London: Atlantic Books – lessons learnt when developing the Bromley-by-Bow Centre in London, for example 'Social entrepreneurs are not public sector people who have just put on a private sector hat – this does not encourage change'.

Co-operatives UK (2011) *Simply Governance* – a comprehensive guide to understanding the systems and processes concerned with the running of a sustainable community enterprise, downloadable from www.uk.coop/sites/default/files/uploads/attachments/coopsuk_simplygovernance_webdownload_0_0.pdf (Accessed 6 March 2017).

Goff, Clare (2016) *Creating Good City Economies In The UK*. A report from The Centre for Local Economic Strategies and The New Economics Foundation, downloadable from https://cles.org.uk/our-work/publications/creating-good-city-economies-in-the-uk/ (Accessed 15 September 2017) A different approach bringing the economic and the social much closer together, making better use of the economic resources already available, and not just relevant to cities alone – check it out.

7

Sustainable Development III: Physical Regeneration

What You See Is What You Get!

'Seeing is believing' – a lot of people won't accept change for the better unless they can see it with their own eyes. We need to carry the whole community with us, and some need to see physical change – now read on ...

Physical Regeneration

This is the most visible part of change, as against economic and social regeneration that don't display their benefits quite as openly. Consequently physical regeneration attracts a greater share of attention, particularly it has to be said where public plaudits are sought by politicians, because most people will only believe regeneration is happening when they see something on the ground.

So identify which aspects of local regeneration can be tied to physical outcomes, and grab people's attention with those, and then add in indicators of the wider benefits of social and economic impacts of what you're doing. In the sense of public perception, physical regeneration is the easy bit, but you must get that right in all respects as a good foundation for the rest of the programme.

Housing

No new houses should be built away from public transport routes – unless of course you ride a horse to the shops.

Sorry, but there it is. Saving the environment begins at home. Building to last for a hundred years and higher than the local flood level (polar ice cap melt-line?) wouldn't hurt either. And don't build on agricultural land, reducing the local capacity to produce food, unless you're 100% sure that imported food (and drink) will always be available and affordable to support your new residents ...

For the rest, housing development is a major element in regeneration. The best approach will vary according to local conditions, and there are many variables:

- Housing developer – either a private firm, a social housing firm (housing association), or a community land trust, and whether or not borrowing the money for the development

- Housing types – flats or houses or both, detached or semi-detached or terraces, numbers of bedrooms

- Housing tenure – for sale or to let

- Percentage of affordable housing (and there are varying definitions of 'affordable', partly depending on whether it's housing for sale or to let. How about 10% of every publicly-owned housing development going to a community land trust? No right to buy = affordable housing to let forever)

- Percentage of social housing for rent (what used to be called 'council housing' in the UK, now 'social housing' under the control of an RSL or 'registered social landlord' such as a housing association), and whether or not 'pepper-potted' around the development rather than in one street

- Environmental standards for house construction (e.g. 'eco-homes') and surrounding space ('public realm')

- Extent and nature of the site – if 'brownfield' not greenfield, what was it used for before?

- Density of the development – how many homes per hectare?

- Match of local housing need to all the above

Your local housing and planning authorities will have all the information (and more) to put numbers to these variables, and can advise you on the range of possible approaches. There are also techniques in laying out housing estates – cul-de-sacs and ring roads have entirely different attributes – and don't forget the impact of new houses on the wider road and services network. Housing is more than somewhere to live – there are design links to health and employment, and also to reducing the conditions for built-in crime (Secured by Design, 2015).

One of the issues in the UK today is the lack of cheap social housing, to rent or to buy – what used to be called 'council housing' when the UK government permitted local councils to build houses. Most social housing is now built and managed by separate organisations called housing associations, but all social housing is now subject to 'right to buy' legislation, which means in practice that as people buy their homes from their social housing landlords, the loss to the pool of social housing is not being replaced. Most local councils have a policy that up to 40% of all new housing must be affordable housing, but if developers show they are making less than 20% profit on the whole development, they can evade these requirements.

One way around this conundrum is the community land trust option, developed in North America and now burgeoning in the UK. The basic principle is that the land itself is secured in community ownership without the possibility of resale – this protects the site from inflationary land values. Houses built on that site can then be let out at affordable rents to local people, and there is no statutory right to buy, so when they move on the housing remains affordable. This is all managed on a community share basis – it is also possible to allow long-time tenants to build up a little equity in their shares, so when they sell them back to the community land trust they have built up a sum towards a deposit on their own house.

If there's any suitable land in your regeneration area, you may consider getting local trustees together to form a community land trust to see what can be achieved – see also the case study at the end of this chapter.

Workspace

For which work, we cry?

'Workspace' is sometimes used colloquially to mean 'managed workspace', i.e. spaces for small firms, often 'incubation units' designed as a starting place for new businesses. In its broader sense the word covers everything from shops to warehouses to factories to offices.

In boom times you will find developers wanting to build workspace first and find occupants second – we've all seen new retail and office blocks with large 'Space to Let' signs, and green fields sprouting developers' adverts. This is about investing capital to cater for a perceived 'market', but are we talking about real need or an un-researched future? There will be an opportunity cost (and possibly a white elephant) if workspace is built where there is no demand.

A more cautious approach matches the benefits of the location with economic opportunities and defines spaces by business needs, for example:

- Floor area/building size

- Nearness to transport network or parking

- Nearness to related businesses (shops work well together as a group of them attracts more customers)

- Nearness to potential labour force

- Power supply (some industrial processes need special '3-Phase electricity' to run the machines) and other services

- 'Broadband' computer links to the Internet (by the by, what will happen to the Internet if there isn't enough electricity to run the computers?)

This approach can be matched by research into actual firms who might use these spaces (see pro forma in Appendix 4).

Be prepared for some local debate about the best location for different types of workspace, and remember a simple shortage of types of space is not of itself a reason to build some more, where is the demand? Does the space in question need other local services to sustain it? Incubation units in particular will need one or more local organisations to provide business support and advice for budding enterprises before they can succeed.

Eyesores

One of the more depressing sights in the world is old commercial buildings for which there is no modern use. Converting old buildings – for work or for housing – will almost certainly be more expensive than building new, particularly if the current owner has an inflated idea of the building's value!

Local people will be glad to see these eyesores removed one way or another – and it's better for business, as well as local morale – so if you have such derelict sites, make it a priority to find a future for them, which almost certainly means finding a private investor. This has been another major focus of regeneration, and you will find a choice of experts to help you review possibilities (see Masterplanning in Chapter 8).

But as ever, don't be so desperate to get rid of eyesores that you let your other standards drop. There was a proposal to convert a derelict public house in our village into 35 homes but with only 17 parking spaces 'because it's in an urban area'. Mitcheldean is a village surrounded by countryside!

Such a development would have exacerbated the already problematic parking in the village, and our objections based on that issue were upheld, so the empty building is still there looking for a new owner.

Public Realm

Traditionally this has been about road and paving surfaces, with a side helping of disabled access – in fact, design guides for open air places where everyone goes.

As we start to regenerate places with everyone in mind, there are other aspects of life which can usefully be brought into the public realm pantheon:

- Play facilities for young people of all ages
- Public art
- Public seats, particularly with elderly walkers in mind
- Cycle racks
- Health walks
- Trees and green areas
- Public toilets and baby change facilities

I'm always struck by architects' impressions of new shopping developments and public squares, they always seem to be full of smart 30-something men and women carrying shopping bags – no kids, no grannies, no wheelchairs, no beggars. Let's pretend all of life is important, shall we? And won't it be better for the local economy if everyone enjoys their visit to the shops?

One trend that seems to be sweeping the public realm these days, though the idea has been around for a long time, is the concept of 'shared space' – nice open-looking areas with low speed limits that vehicles and pedestrians can jointly occupy. You will need to check whether this approach would work in your area – it can work well in low-speed low-volume streets like residential cul-de-sacs, but not so well on main roads where vehicle drivers can feel they are still the most important users to the detriment of the needs of the 10% of us who are blind or partially sighted, and other people who need more formal road-crossing arrangements.

One example of shared space at the Kimbrose Triangle in Gloucester is currently the focus of campaigning groups seeking the reinstallation of a formal pedestrian crossing, as without kerbs or different-textured paviors for orientation, together with an audible 'traffic stopping' signal, blind people in particular are feeling at risk when crossing what is actually a main road. Of course anything that separates out the different road users, including different surface treatments as shown in the photograph, rather destroys the shared space concept anyway.

Kimbrose Triangle shared space

Leisure

Eight hours sleeping, eight hours working, eight hours playing? Sounds like a mythical ideal – particularly if you have a large family or other commitments, such as two or more jobs to make ends meet.

I won't attempt to list all the many ways people choose to take a break, but get some statistics for your local area. Clearly, 'leisure' is an important part of quality of life (and local culture), but bear in mind that some people have money to spend on enjoyment and some don't, so free opportunities – libraries, parks, learning opportunities – are as important as facilities that charge admission.

And dare I state the obvious – be careful of committing capital to something without rigorous business planning. For example, skateboarding areas have proved remarkably resilient in the UK, but some other ventures have proved to be white elephants and require continual revenue subsidies to stay open. Best leave expensive facilities to the private sector, but always beware of 'opportunity cost', when you could have done something else with a space that would have given greater benefit to local people if used in a different way.

Brownfield and Greenfield

'Brownfield' land is simply land that has been built on or used before, not necessarily very long ago. As we have become more concerned about saving the planet, a greater emphasis has been placed on redeveloping brownfield land rather than taking up fresh 'greenfield' land that has never seen a brick or any extensive human activity.

I always think of Singapore when this issue comes up. Singapore is an island that has been developed over 200 years, and I remember from the 1970s a complete mixture of green areas and modern buildings, though I'm told it's more built up now. Maybe West London is a better example, with its plentiful green parks – nice, if more for humans than wildlife – but should everywhere end up like that? Better than Athens perhaps, which is almost 100% buildings, and dust is left on cars every time it rains.

There has been a UK policy for some years of keeping a 'green belt' around towns and cities, but that has come into question as the government seeks places to build new homes to meet the projected population expansion. For example, the view from London seems to be that Cheltenham and Gloucester 120 miles away are one urban area, but this view has not been shared by the families keen to keep farming in the few miles of green belt between the two towns. The fact that it is usually easier to develop greenfield sites than brownfield sites, where past usage for other purposes can throw up so-called 'abnormals', such as dealing with contaminated land, that add to development costs, just makes the debate more intense.

So when faced with this kind of decision, weigh up the alternatives. Balance an appreciation of the positive contribution the green fields in question will make to the quality of local life (local food production?) against the

positive contribution of the proposed development. While losing some agricultural land may not compare with the destruction of the Brazilian rain forests, it's only a difference of degree – it's a local decision with a global resonance, and they're all (rightly) controversial.

There's no one answer, I'm afraid, and this is the first of many areas where simple model-watching will not produce the right result. How about requiring reclaimed agricultural land or recreated wildlife habitat of the same extent as the green fields being built on? West London or no?

Archaeology

'Regeneration' implies something has gone before.

Not everything above or below ground will be historically significant, but it may be important to local people.

Archaeology as a science is something over 100 years old, and as with many sciences, you don't have to be an archaeologist to understand the technical reports (go for the 'executive summary' at the front or the conclusions at the back).

That's useful, because if you are redeveloping a historic town or country area you will need to have your facts straight about what you are building on.

We're not necessarily talking about putting anything found on display. Since the heady days of rescue archaeology in the 1970s, it has become perfectly acceptable to preserve things underground, such as the Shakespearean Rose Theatre in London now safely under a modern basement since its discovery during building work in 1989 and scheduling as an ancient monument in 1992.

Archaeology is not just about old architecture of course, but also about roads, field boundaries, cemeteries, rubbish heaps and working sites from the industrial era back to the Iron Age, all of which can have an effect on what you're doing.

> Investigating these things can take a little time, so build it into your plans early - one project redeveloping a college built over an old Roman site was put back several months because the college authorities wouldn't allow holes to be dug on campus while the students were around to fall into them ...

Underground

Not that one. No, not that one either.

I'm talking about things in the ground that can get in the way of regeneration schemes, and I'm told are the single largest cause of increased costs in new development schemes. This is particularly true of brownfield land, where there may be ground contamination underneath old buildings and factories, but is also true of greenfield land, where apart from underground tunnels in old mining areas, there may be natural caves, geological faults, and other traps connected to the nature of the soil, and groundwater levels.

So don't assume everything underground is fine for your purposes – as with archaeology, check it out early.

Design

This is not just a matter of aesthetics, what things look like – always contentious – but don't forget:

- Functionality (what does it do?)

- Fit for purpose (is this the best way to achieve what you want?)

- Sustainability (will it last?)

- Value for money

- Value for materials and labour, as even contributions in kind can be wasted

And of course ...

- Budget, including cash flow (how quick can we finish the job?)

Usefully, these vital factors can also help resolve arguments about the look of the thing!

There are some particular environmental concerns around sustainability, such as 'carbon zero' – producing things in such a way and with such materials that don't release more carbon dioxide into the atmosphere, either when making them or when using them. Minimising waste is another useful principle. Improved house design and construction to save energy in response to climate change can also mean people save on their heating bills, which is particularly important for people that are struggling financially – good value all round.

There are regularly updated design guidelines you can research and apply, not least for the built environment, and some of which are a requirement of UK public funding, for example:

- Code for Sustainable Homes – launched by the UK government in 2007 and still valid for current schemes but withdrawn for future developments

- The more recent Home Quality Mark, a new voluntary housing standard developed by BRE Global Ltd (2015)

- BREEAM (Building Research Establishment Environmental Assessment Method) aimed at making sure other types of buildings are also environmentally-friendly (BRE Global Ltd, 2014)

- CEEQUAL (Civil Engineering Environmental Quality assessment and awards scheme) (CEEQUAL Ltd, 2015), now being delivered by BRE Global Ltd

- NICE – National Institute for Health and Care Excellence provide a range of guidelines for health benefit, and have a new guideline in preparation – Housing: Planning to Improve Health and Wellbeing

- Secured by Design – guidance from the UK police force on how to build in community safety – I've heard a story of one developer who ignored police advice and was accused of creating a 'criminal landscape' as a result!

Final health warning – designing logos: if you can't avoid the discussion altogether, for sanity's sake have it at the *end* of a meeting ...

Case Study: Lydden Meadow Community Land Trust

This is a story of how a small community got together to solve their local housing shortage – what worked well, what not so well and what advice they would give to others facing the same issue.

In 2005 an open village meeting in Buckland Newton, Dorset (population including surrounding hamlets of around 600 residents) registered concerns over high house prices and the resulting impact on local villagers' ability to live and work locally – a common concern in many parts of rural Britain – along with the decline in school numbers. This raised the idea that if the village could acquire land cheaply then it could build houses itself at a cost which ought to be within the reach of locals.

In 2006 a group of volunteers decided to use a Community Land Trust model to acquire land and set up a trust that could build all the affordable houses needed by the village. An advert was placed in the local newspaper for landowners willing to offer a piece of land adjacent to the designated village area for a price that was better than agricultural prices, but well below development land prices. This produced an offer of five possible options which were considered by the planners at West Dorset District Council and resulted in two options being brought before another village meeting in February 2007, with the result that the piece of land now occupied by Lydden Meadow was voted as the favoured option.

Lydden Meadow housing development

Because the land was within the Dorset Area of Outstanding Natural Beauty (AONB), the planners insisted on a sympathetic design based on the concept of a farmhouse and converted farm buildings around a central farmyard space. The Buckland Newton Community Property Trust (BNCPT) negotiated a development loan from the District Council for the estimated build costs plus land purchase, along with a grant from the Tudor Trust of £40,000 for implementing an innovative build method. Initially a straw bale design was chosen for the houses, very sustainable, cheap to construct and environmentally friendly, but there were many downsides, chief among which were the inability to get finance for mortgages and insurance, and despite planning permission this build plan failed in April 2008.

The Trust had established the need for 10 affordable houses with the help of a parish survey, but was now faced with a major rethink about how to

(Continued)

(Continued)

develop them. A revised building estimate found that the cost of constructing eco-friendly houses with very low running costs ran way ahead of the villagers' ability to afford them. The Trust decided, after so much work, to at least have a go at seeking further grant funding. A huge effort was spent in talking to the government's Homes and Communities Agency (HCA) which resulted finally in an offer of a £750,000 grant, albeit with a number of conditions, including:

- Abiding by best practice as a landlord, fulfilling all legal and other obligations

- Sub-contracting housing management and rent collection to an accredited housing management company (currently Magna Housing Group)

- A high degree of home insulation

- Choosing house colours from a range of options provided

West Dorset District Council were also very supportive, and provided a loan of £1.4m repayable over 25 years at a rate of 4.9%. Current projections suggest this loan will be paid off within 12 years, but the option remains to extend the loan against any other approved local project.

In the spring of 2010, with the promise of funding in place, the Trust set out on serious negotiations with the appointed builder, CG Fry & Son. Not surprisingly, with Fry's high build standards they suggested significant design improvements that could be achieved for the same price, leading to a considerably re-engineered layout that markedly increased energy efficiency. Planning for the new proposal was granted in July 2010 with stringent conditions on drainage, flood prevention, environmental improvements and exterior materials.

Building started in early September 2010 and was completed in mid-summer 2011, with all 10 houses being awarded the stringent Code 4 building certification, which included suitable access for wheelchairs, a heat exchange heating system and rainwater recycling for low running cost. In addition, a communal wildflower meadow was sown and a footbridge built across the river. The Trust finally took possession of the completed development from the builders on 29 July 2011.

The names and number of applicants for these houses had ebbed and flowed over time, and in autumn 2010 the Trust embarked on an advertising campaign to ensure that all eligible applicants with a strong connection to the village had a chance to put their names forward. The difficult task of allocating homes in a fair and transparent manner was helped by advice from the Housing Department of the District Council, and resulted in five houses being offered to villagers on a tenancy basis and five on a shared ownership basis (one at 40% private ownership, one at 28% and three others at 25%).

The overwhelming criteria for allocation were a connection via birth, long residency or work to the village, and an understanding that the properties would never end up on the open market – the Trust holds these homes and the land on which they are built in perpetuity, so the village will always own all or part of each property.

Jon Sulkin, currently one of the eight trustees, identifies three critical factors in the project's success:

1. The availability of the land (previously farmland) at a sensible price

2. The substantial grant support, itself based on an effective business plan

3. The way the working group organised themselves

This last point is not so much about the choice of constitution for the Trust, but the group being clear about their objectives, about the methodology of the development, and having a clear spread of responsibilities so there was no competition over who was managing what part of the scheme! This principle continues, as trustees with financial, architectural and company secretary roles and experience manage those parts of the business, while two other trustees are available to handle more general phone calls.

The Trust has also benefitted from very good working relationships with their construction partners, CG Fry & Son, and their housing management partners, Magna Housing Group. Local tradespeople are used for any maintenance issues, and once the District Council loan is paid off, there will be a rental income that can be used to support the village in other ways.

Further Reading

Ferber, Uwe; Grimski, Detlef; Millar, Kate and Nathanail, Paul (2006) *Sustainable Brownfield Regeneration*. A report for CABERNET (Concerted Action on Brownfield and Economic Regeneration Network) published by the University of Nottingham – a broad, practical review of the topic – downloadable from www.palgo.org/files/CABERNET%20Network%20Report%202006.pdf (Accessed 14 June 2017). Dr Nathanail has more recently published his own book on the subject.

Hubel, Vello and Lussow, Diedra (1984) *Focus on Designing*. Toronto: McGraw-Hill Ryerson Ltd – there are a number of books on designing, but I liked the practical approach of this one.

Chartered Institution of Highways & Transportation (2010) *Manual for Streets* 2 – downloadable from www.ciht.org.uk/en/document-summary/index.cfm/docid/

055693F6-8DB0-4BBE-AA9FF1B5BC5E9412 (Accessed 14 June 2017). An extension of the UK government's *Manual for Streets* (2007) explaining how the original principles can be applied more widely, covering among other things the concept of shared space.

House of Commons Women and Equalities Committee (2017) *Building for Equality: Disability and the Built Environment*, Ninth Report of Session 2016–17. London: House of Commons.

8
Planning

Now, we're ready to look at the 'how' of what we want to achieve – and not before time, says you.

First Steps

You may have inherited a regeneration programme for your local area, but what if you're starting one from scratch?

We've already mentioned the SWOT analysis (see Chapter 1), which will give you some themes to focus on and some individual project ideas to chew over. There will probably also be a range of regeneration approaches already tried in places near you or communities similar to yours, and the people concerned will be happy to tell you what worked for them and what didn't. If your local council can't steer you towards them, try one of the UK organisations listed at the back of the book.

Getting an early view of your own area from an outside expert has its advantages, as not only will you benefit from their expertise, but their report will give local people something to agree and disagree with, and so start effective discussions about priorities. There are private sector regeneration consultants, but also some national organisations such as Locality who can offer you consultancy services from experienced people in the voluntary sector. Prices can range from £50,000 for a survey report and regeneration framework for a small market town to several hundred thousand for a major city – make sure you get value for money.

There are some UK models for doing it yourself, for example:

- Parish Plans – a fairly well-established approach in rural areas, once linked to the UK planning process – ask your local council for help, or search the web for models and advice (see Countryside Agency, 2004)

- The BIMBY (Beauty In My Back Yard) Housing Toolkit – available online (www.bimby.org.uk) from the Prince's Foundation for Building Communities

- Transition Initiatives – a way of bringing people together to review all aspects of local living (www.transitionnetwork.org)

There have been other toolkits in the past, such as Planning For Real, a long-standing map-based community planning approach which is still available but on a consultancy basis only, rather than a simple purchase. There was also a Market Towns Health Check developed in England by the Countryside Agency in 2002, which was developed into a Market Towns Healthcheck Handbook published by the now-dissolved Action for Market Towns in 2005 – there are a thousand market towns in England alone.

For all of these approaches – whether you're customising your own or auditing somebody else's – check that the coverage is sufficiently rigorous:

- Have the public, private and voluntary sector all been involved, particularly those who own key sites?

- Have all groups within the local community been involved? Young people in particular tend not to come to public meetings with older people

- Have all the elements in the 'Sustainable Communities' list in Chapter 5 been addressed?

Whichever approach you take, you should end up with a list of proposed local projects or actions, some of which may already have begun, some will be new proposals based on ideas from residents, and some suggested by consultants or other outside sources based on experience elsewhere. All of these proposals should have the following detail:

- Brief project description

- Contact details for the person leading the project

- Note of project partners/people who need to be involved

- Estimated costs, including any money still to find

- Timetable with an estimated completion date

- Measurable results – expected outputs and outcomes

Everything that comes up in these planning processes will be important to someone, and so not to be excluded out of hand. There is a question of what is to be tackled first, however, both in terms of how long each proposal will take to complete, and also whether the end result offers good value for the time and money to be expended.

You will probably find only a small percentage of proposals are ready to go in every respect, and these will inevitably become your first priorities. Some good ideas simply have to wait their time - for example, we knew from the outset that there was a gap in the Lake District youth hostelling chain at Ulverston, but the right people and location didn't come along until seven years after the Ulverston regeneration project had started.

If you have absolutely no resources to start with, there is still an argument for producing a range of proposals (see Project Appraisal in Chapter 11), both as part of a bid for resources, and also to be prepared when funding opportunities come up, as money tends to become available for one particular area, such as education, rather than for any purpose you choose.

Good luck!

Market Research

Whether you're talking about a social, economic or physical regeneration proposal, you will need to make sure – if you want it to have a long life – that the demand for it is sufficient to ensure it garners the necessary revenue, rental income and wider support in years to come.

A lot of 'jolly good ideas' don't actually stand up on their own financially, and may need to be 'buddied' with something else in order to survive.

Much of this will come up during project appraisal (see Chapter 11), but you may have to employ classic research techniques (or a researcher) to come up with a definitive answer before you embed a proposal in your overall regeneration programme. These techniques can include:

- Research into potential competition, e.g. in the case of a new youth hostel, what other campsites, hostels or cheap hotels are nearby, and how they are doing both socially and commercially

- Desk research into numbers of potential beneficiaries, e.g. local demographics, visitor numbers to nearby hostels, appeal and visitor numbers of other local attractions

- Literature search for any relevant recent studies, e.g. local tourism strategies

- Survey of actual demand – more difficult when you're taking about visitors from further afield than a quick survey of local residents – ask youth hostelling organisations for their help and advice

Confirming demand is good due diligence when drawing up a regeneration programme. And as ever – don't assume – check!

Town Planning

This became a feature of life as soon as people began crowding into towns from the countryside. Ancient Rome had shopping malls, and Pompeii had pedestrian crossings that slowed the traffic.

There have been a number of trends in more modern times:

- New towns to deal with population pressure

- Ring roads, car parks and bypasses to cater for the omnipotent motor car

- Planning zones to make sure there was space for both housing and employment

- 'Mixed use' planning when travelling some distance to work went out of favour

Now we are hearing about 'eco-towns' full of 'eco-houses', and otherwise complete communities – the cynics might say this is just new towns writ large, with a green veil over government desire to build more houses in the countryside.

You get the idea – town planning looks like a flavour-of-the-month science, but as a discipline it has been and still is striving to find the best programmable solutions. Meanwhile developers have been coming in with their own cost-effective ideas, one of the latest being 'permeable' sites that people move through freely. There you go.

Best idea for a regeneration worker – get to know your local government planning officer. Be aware they have formal training, much experience and a fair amount of clout. Work with them to make sense of the mass of historical data and conflicting opportunities, but they may be more into plans than development, so be prepared for a major influencing exercise if you have new proposals to share.

Spatial Planning

This is what is currently called at local government level in the UK the Local Plan or the Local Development Plan – all district or unitary authorities must have one, overseen by the planning officer mentioned above. This is a strategic document noting in some detail the housing, workplace, and other such development objectives and guidelines for the local government area, as a touchstone for use when reviewing any new development proposals. As such, your regeneration plans would do well to fit into the overall Local Plan – make it a priority to identify any proposals that don't fit in, as these will need more careful handling if they are to come to fruition.

The Local Plan in England refers upwards to the National Planning Policy Framework, published by the government in March 2012 to provide 'a balanced set of national planning policies for England covering the economic, social and environmental aspects of development'(Department for Communities and Local Government, 2012).

A major feature of the Framework was the introduction of 'a presumption in favour of sustainable development', intended to ensure that local planning authorities identified and planned for the development which their areas needed. The Framework makes it clear that applications that will deliver sustainable development should normally be allowed – but in practice the definition of 'sustainable development' used is not the broad theoretical one as described in this book, but rather one bounded by official policies and the requirements placed on those applying for planning permission.

For example, environmental impact studies are a regular requirement of planning applications, but economic impact assessments are not (yet) officially defined or required to the same extent. Carbon footprint is more of an official issue than a balanced local economy, which is why (for example) controlling what kind of shops open in your town is by no means easy.

There used to be English regional strategies that lay between national and local planning frameworks, but these have now been removed except for the London Plan. Other parts of the UK have their own political assemblies or parliaments, and so have their own planning strategies to inform Local Plans. Northern Ireland has its Regional Development Strategy (Department for Regional Development, 2012), and *Planning Policy Wales* sets out the land use planning policies of the Welsh Assembly (Welsh Government, 2016), while the *Wales Spatial Plan People, Places, Futures* sets a strategic framework to guide future development (Welsh Government, 2008). In Scotland, there is the National Planning Framework for Scotland (Scottish Government, 2014a) and the published *Scottish Planning Policy*, with strategic plans required for the four main city-regions of Aberdeen, Dundee, Edinburgh and Glasgow (Scottish Government, 2014b).

Many years ago, I was lucky to meet a group of women from Russia, coming to our community environment project in Hampshire to see how they might set up similar schemes of their own. I was told that under the Soviet Union there had been no independent planning policy or control, factories were just put where the state needed them. Also, there was no charity law, to support the development of individual community initiatives, and any meeting of more than three people that wasn't a meeting of the Communist Party was illegal.

The UK may be particular in having a long history of planning control, but wherever you are, check out what the official local government plans say for your area and make contact with the people who write and approve them. If they already underscore what you want to do, all the better – get local government on your side.

Neighbourhood Planning

Since the Localism Act was passed in 2011, there has been the prospect of locally-created 'neighbourhood development plans' (NDPs) in England to form an official part of Local Development Frameworks. Many of these are carried out by English parish councils using their parish boundaries as area borders, though it is also possible for community groups (with permission from the local planning authority) to develop their own plans, even ones that cross a number of parish boundaries. These are a good example of what this book is about – shared action to plan a better future for your local community.

These neighbourhood development plans are validated at the end of the creative process by a referendum of all residents within the plan area. Consequently, it is good practice (as ever) to involve local people from the outset, and to regularly publicise the emerging conclusions. Get in touch with your local planning authority, who will be able to give you general guidance, and hopefully direct you not only to an expert to lead you through the process, but also to sources of government funding to pay for the whole exercise.

The process can take up to two years, and some regular stages or steps are becoming established (see Table 8.1), with many thanks to Gloucestershire Rural Community Council for their advice to the author's parish council, and the Campaign to Protect Rural England (CPRE) and the National Association of Local Councils (NALC) for their published guidance.

Why go to all this trouble, particularly when these plans are not permitted to contradict policies of the higher-level Local Plans?

One advantage of neighbourhood development plans is that while a higher-level plan may say there should be so many houses built in the ensuing five years, the NDP can define exactly where these should be built and, potentially more important, where they should *not* be built. Even draft NDPs have proved critical to local decisions about planning permission, such as a proposal for 200 new houses near Lydney in the Forest of Dean which the draft Lydney NDP helped to deflect.

The potential power of NDPs – the best opportunity local people have to influence the planning process in England – is shown by the readiness of housing developers to challenge them if they are not seen to be securely evidence-based or not the product of a rigorous process. The more exacting the process employed, with checks at every stage, the more effective the plan will be – and don't forget to include a review date to ensure the plan remains valid in the light of future changes of any kind.

As you will appreciate, a neighbourhood development plan can provide a ready-made and community-approved framework for a local regeneration programme.

Table 8.1

	STEPS	ACTION
1	Getting started	Discuss the idea locally to gain general approval, select the preferred 'neighbourhood area' for the plan (often a parish), identify key partners including landowners, set up a steering group and agree an action plan, and formally apply to the local planning authority for permission to go forward
2	Identifying issues	Start building an evidence base (critical to final approval) with the demographic and planning information already available, augment it with a mapping exercise on the character of the neighbourhood area, seek advice from the planning authority on the need for environmental and other such assessments
3	Developing a vision and objectives	Community consultation (a public event works well) to display evidence gathered so far and ask for views on local issues and ideas, use the feedback to develop a vision for the neighbourhood area and objectives for the plan
4	Generate and test options/solutions	Explore options and solutions to address key issues and achieve the vision in the context of the baseline information and public opinion, check them with relevant landowners as well as higher-level planning policies, and carry out a second consultation on your choices
5	Drafting the NDP	Decide the plan layout (there are several published now to view as models), draft planning policies and guidance and check they conform to higher-level plans as well as the needs of equality and diversity
6	Pre-submission consultation and submission of the plan	A third and final consultation to confirm the plan meets what the community wants, make any final changes and then submit to the local planning authority
7	Independent examination	The planning authority will send the plan out for independent external assessment, which may lead to final refinements
8	Referendum and the 'making' of the NDP	If the referendum says 'Yes' (only a simple majority of the vote is required) the plan is then 'made' by the local planning authority and joins their suite of planning documents

(CPRE, 2012: 21–48)

Land Use Planning

This section is about another level, land use or development planning, and in particular planning permission for individual sites. A number of people (usually elected local councillors supported by planning officers) make decisions about new proposals, either for a new development or building conversion, or occasionally for a planning policy to guide future development.

This is one of the darkest parts of the regeneration jungle, inhabited by strange tribes, such as:

- The traditional jobs-at-all-costs tribe

- The timid investment-at-all-costs tribe

- The predictable make-a-change-to-show-who's-boss tribe

- The proud I-walk-with-developers tribe

- The rare what-does-good practice-say tribe

- The unrelated what-does-it-say-in-the-book tribe

And several more you might name.

You may have clear talks about the options for your area from the outset, and talk about refinements afterwards, but in between you are in the jungle surrounded by warring tribes. This means you will need:

- A good local guide to introduce you to the tribes

- Good preparation – don't rush in, prepare your approaches

- Patience to influence more than one tribe at once

It may take some time to see your way clear to your objective, getting your planning proposal through or stopping one that's not going to be helpful. When negotiating with the tribes don't forget your mission (but remember what can happen to unsuccessful missionaries). And you'll probably find members of these tribes in England's new Local Enterprise Partnerships too – it's a jungle, guys.

Masterplanning

This is the process of translating local regeneration planning into physical maps, usually with various levels of stakeholder participation, and often as a prelude to marketing sites to developers, or otherwise putting physical regeneration work out to tender – what at a strategic level can be called a 'regeneration framework', and in engineering terms is called a 'conceptual model' (thanks, bro).

Several professional skills will need to be brought together, such as urban design, landscape architecture, transport planning, civil engineering and commercial development. Depending on the size of your regeneration area and the complexity of your objectives, you should expect to have a consortium of experts preparing the masterplan with you.

That being the case, as well as the usual processes of checking people's past work and the quality of their communication (see Tendering in Chapter 11), be prepared to have someone chair the whole exercise so that everyone – locals and experts alike – is properly involved in the right way and at the right time. If you're the local regeneration worker, it's your responsibility to make sure the plans make sense. Here are some tips, with many thanks to urban designer Matt Lally:

1. Keep a focus on outcomes, what you are trying to achieve, in social and economic as well as physical terms

2. Adopt an evidence-based approach informed by what has been proven to work elsewhere … but balance this with local appropriateness and innovation (novel ideas – not replicating what someone else has done before, that's fashion)

3. Avoid the false dichotomy between people and place – use masterplanning as a means of integration

4. Effective community engagement early saves time and money later

5. Have strong governance structures from the outset, i.e. who's on the steering group for the masterplan, and how will they work together to deliver proposals?

6. Effective public and private sector engagement from the outset – the 'visioning' phase – will result in aligning a host of funding streams and programmes

7. Smooth the planning process – have strong links to local planning officers and decision-makers, both for clarity and for confidence that the masterplan will actually happen

8. Keep continuity of involvement – this grows confidence in the whole team to deliver

9. Relationships matter most – great places don't just happen, they are created and nurtured by committed and talented people working together

10. View yourself as a catalyst

And don't assume that hired contractors will automatically cover the whole brief. Once as part of a regeneration framework steering group I learned a lot about 'culture', not because the consultants taught me, but because in the absence of ready-made information I researched local cultural issues on their behalf, otherwise that part of the finished study would have been rather sparse.

Innovation

Regeneration is about change, and so we should expect to find new solutions for new or old or even for future issues.

This does not mean copying what may have worked elsewhere – that's fashion, and how sure are you that your place is exactly the same as that other one? From first principles, I'd be equally sure it wasn't!

Innovation means thinking outside the box – so-called 'blue sky' thinking – and so by definition new ideas – or new applications for old ideas – can come from the unlikeliest quarters, and perhaps are more likely to come from ordinary people than from experts who may be hidebound by past experience or by industry standards (incidentally, if mere rules and regulations get in the way, I suggest you change 'em!).

A full third of the regeneration projects in Cinderford came from local residents, for example, not from anywhere else. Having said that, expert advice was then needed to make sure these visions could become a reality. Repopulating the empty 'Triangle' in Cinderford with shops, public space, toilets and a clock tower involved a whole host of specialists by the finish.

One of Ulverston's brown tourism signs on the main road directing visitors to car parks in the town centre

Turning to the rules – brown tourism signs pointing drivers towards tourist attractions are a familiar sight in the UK, but in the past they were only approved by the local highways authority if they could direct drivers towards places with a car park. This was a great frustration to three visitor attractions in Ulverston in the South Lakes, not least to the world's only Laurel and Hardy Museum (Stan Laurel was born in Ulverston in 1890), which were very popular but didn't have car parks. I spoke to the highways authority and said, how about if we directed cars to the town car parks, where there could be fingerpost signs directing visitors to these attractions? The authority agreed – the pedestrian signs went in – and the three visitor attractions celebrated together with champagne when they finally got their brown tourism signs on the main road!

Difficult times can also encourage innovation. For example, we have been able to build 'carbon zero' houses for years, but they have only now come to the fore under the spur of climate change. Move cautiously with novel solutions – get details of good practice from elsewhere by all means, but check how closely your conditions match those where the innovation has succeeded, and garner local support before going public with the idea.

There can be added benefits from innovation in 'driving value' for prospective developments, which will always please potential investors. A derelict mining area was not looking much of a prospect, until someone suggested using the mining spoil to create a lake, and the subsequent excitement around a waterside development made all the difference to bringing in finance. So get people involved, look at the particular benefits of your local place, and then start to wonder.

Transition Initiatives

This is a community-based approach seeking to provide local solutions to a sustainable local future, a process that has been simply called 'localisation'. The key factor in regeneration terms is 'local resilience' – the capacity of local communities to deal with change. Rob Hopkins in his *Transition Handbook* identifies three main features of resilience:

1. **Diversity** – a range of local people and businesses, a range of land uses with no reliance on one single industry, all provide greater flexibility in dealing with threats and challenges to a local area

2. **Modularity** – less dependence on other networks, for example a range of local provision such as local abattoirs and credit systems provides more resilience in dealing with any disruption in regional, national and international provision such as food distribution and banking

3. **Tightness of feedbacks** – more localised systems will give quicker warning of any failures than national or international systems, where the knock-on effects of poor decisions may not become apparent for some time

(Hopkins, 2008: 55–7)

Rob is leading a real-life application of the Transition movement in the town of Totnes in the county of Devon in England, where one classic example of a loss of past resilience is shown by a local market garden that was covered by a car park in the 1980s. A summary of what can be achieved through localisation is given in the Energy Descent Action Plan for Totnes:

Localisation is a powerful concept. Clearly Totnes cannot become self-sufficient, nor would it want to be. It will never be able to make computers or frying pans. However, as the oral history section of this report shows, it used to be far more self-reliant than it is today, functioning far more like a bucket than its present day leaky sieve. There is significant potential for Totnes and District to, for example:

- Produce most of its food locally, and create a range of livelihoods, processing and value-adding that food in the locality

- Source a significant proportion of its building materials, for both new build and retrofits, either from the local area or from recycling from the local waste stream

- Buy its energy from locally owned and managed energy companies rather than distant ones

- Maintain and enhance the proportion of shops in the town that are locally owned, and avoid the 'Ghost Town Britain' phenomenon seen in so many High Streets across the country

- Bring land for development into community ownership, so that the financial gains from that development accrue to the community, rather than to speculative developers

- Make medicines using local plants to treat common ailments

- Use its food wastes to create bio-methane to power vehicles

- Use local currencies and local investment mechanisms to enable more money to be invested in the immediate area

None of this will happen by accident, it needs careful planning and design.

(Hodgson with Hopkins, 2010: 18)

Many other places are also catching this enthusiasm – Transition is now active in 50 countries around the world, thousands of communities, with 34 countries already having a national hub organisation (see www.transition

network.org). There is a guide to starting Transition in your locality – *The Essential Guide to Doing Transition* – which summarises an approach that is still developing:

> Transition is a movement that has been growing since 2005. It is about communities stepping up to address the big challenges they face by starting local. By coming together, they are able to create solutions together. They seek to nurture a caring culture, one focused on connection with self, others and nature. They are reclaiming the economy, sparking entrepreneurship, reimagining work, reskilling themselves and weaving webs of connection and support. Courageous conversations are being had; extraordinary change is unfolding.
>
> (Transition Network Team, 2016: 8)

The sheer excitement of this working together to make a real difference to local living sounds like effective joined-up regeneration to me, with the added bonus of a natural focus on local capacity building – check it out.

Case Study: Cirencester Town Council, Approach to Planning

Parish and town councils in England have no veto on planning applications, though they have a say – such matters are usually decided by district councils or unitary councils who are the local planning authorities. However, even without the prospect of a neighbourhood development plan for their parish, which has some statutory weight, there are other things that town and parish councils can do which are of help when planning the future of their place and also when dealing with potential developers.

And by inference, if you are managing a regeneration programme in a local area, you can encourage your local council (if they are not already involved) to help you to prepare the ground in advance.

Cirencester Town Council in Gloucestershire has taken this proactive approach, with the help of planning consultant Andrea Pellegram, on the basis that taking the lead in thinking about planning matters and raising the profile of the community's response will encourage developers to come to you first. This can lead to useful conversations even before a planning application for a new development is submitted.

Their approach taken can be described as a number of incremental steps:

- Vision for Cirencester – in 2007 the town council began an initiative called 'Our Future Cirencester', working with local residents and businesses to agree what the future of the town should be

(Continued)

(Continued)

- Our Future Cirencester Community Plan – this document built on the vision to provide more detail on local needs and aspirations, and how they might be met, including projects to be led from within the community itself. The plan has four key themes, saying 'Our Future Cirencester' will be:

  o a sustainable market town

  o a good place to grow up

  o an attractive town to live in, visit and where we can enjoy vibrant culture

  o a better place to do business

- Planning Concept Statement – a clear presentation of the development principles defining the kind of place that new developments should produce, with the first declaration being that 'Development must reinforce the strong local identity of Cirencester and not erode the unique qualities and character of the town'

- Planning Policy Statement – the next stage on, expressing community views through planning policy, and providing an evidence base and reference point for use when responding to future planning applications. The statement has been prepared as if it were a neighbourhood plan, and has 50 pages of policies with supporting material under three themes: Growth must complement the town; Quality of design, and of life; and Links, movement and accessibility

- Local Design Code – landscape architects Portus & Whitton have prepared a Design Code for the public realm of Cirencester, an overarching strategy to refer to when considering future streetscape works within the town, whether they be by the public or private sector. The Design Code is intended to provide a practical overview with illustrations to help to recognise and develop the town's historic and future character by bringing a consistent approach to the design and layout of the town's streets

The town clerk recalls that the extra benefits from this whole approach included building local trust and credibility, not only within the town, but when speaking to developers and also the local planning authority, Cotswold District Council, as they prepared their statutory Local Plan. One definitive outcome has been the ability to ask a particular developer to phase in their new houses rather than build them all at once, so as to give the town time to absorb the impact of more residents.

And through this planning process local talent was found, people with the skills and strength of character needed to take on particular tasks. Some of these residents are now key people in the Cirencester Community Development Trust, set up in 2012 and now with charitable status, whose declared aims are:

New paviors in Cirencester marketplace February 2017 – a mixture of traditional kerbs and shared space

- To help to make Cirencester a great place to live

- To assist community development in Cirencester

- To help young people build skills and access opportunity

- To advance the arts and support an understanding of the history and heritage of the town

So there has been further benefit from this planning approach, leading almost directly into community-based regeneration in practice.

Further Reading

Cheshire Community Action (2014) *Introduction to Parish Plans* – a good introduction to the topic – downloadable from www.cheshireaction.org.uk/uploads/documents/Intro-Guide-Parish-Plans.pdf (Accessed 14 June 2017).

Luigi Russi (2015) *Everything Gardens and Other Stories: Growing Transition Culture*. Plymouth: University of Plymouth Press – a good update on the Transition movement.

9

Regeneration Management

Once you've established your team of locals and specialists (see Chapter 2, Team Work), and begun planning your approach (see Chapter 8), you will also need to manage the overall exercise while it's happening.

You may be quite relaxed about (politely) giving direction to people more senior and experienced than yourself, or the prospect may terrify you until you've had some practice (see Chapter 12 for more advice on managing yourself and your actions). Just keep in front of you the priorities already agreed by everyone, and stand up for them, using board or steering group meetings for confirmation – even senior people will expect you to do this, and the local community can only really criticise you if you diverge from your declared regeneration objectives. Above all, keep everyone in the area well informed of progress by regular publicity, using newsletters, websites and social media as appropriate.

Programme Management

Managing a lot of related projects that address a collective 'why' – hurrah! (See Chapter 1, Why Regenerate?)

Well I used to think that was it, and in some cases it's true. In other cases, there needs to be interconnected management by a central group of different projects, each delivering parts of a desired whole – such as breaking cycles of deprivation, for instance.

When we started the Oxfordshire programme to identify best practice in breaking cycles of deprivation, there was no published manual or blueprint to tell us how to do it. We had to develop the theory of what we wanted to achieve – a place to work, a place to live – which we did by studying conclusions from other regeneration programmes and producing a combined model that was then approved by our steering group (see Cycles of Deprivation in Chapter 1). Make sure you've got collective approval of the thrust of your regeneration programme, basing it on as much evidence as you can find.

Once you have a clear basis for your regeneration programme, you will be able to assess to what extent various project proposals and ideas fit into it or not. One tool that can help you with this is a basket of indicators to assess overall progress, with targets that may be shared over time between a number of different approaches and actions. In Oxfordshire after much discussion we came up with these 10 measures:

1. Level 4 Maths and English achievement at Key Stage 2 (KS 2 – age 11)

2. Achievement of five or more A*–C grades at GCSE including English and Maths at Key Stage 4 (KS 4 – age 16)

3. Achievement gap between pupils eligible for free school meals and their peers achieving the expected level at KS 2 and 4

4. Anti-social behaviour incidents and repeats

5. Criminal damage

6. Jobseeker's Allowance (unemployment benefit) claimants

7. The percentage of 16- to 18-year-olds not in employment, education or training

8. Income Support claimants (those on low pay)

9. All age, all-cause mortality, from which to calculate local life expectancy

10. Under-18 teenage conceptions

We were able to get a baseline database of these measures for the local government wards in the two programme target areas. However, the problem came in working out an agreed system to tie these overarching indicators to local projects that had their own (quite separate) targeted outputs, many of which had already started, to see which projects gave best value in achieving the overall aim.

This proved too bureaucratic an exercise to share widely – people on the steering group couldn't see how it would work, and in one sense at least they were right – a number of the individual project managers rebelled. So, the lesson from this example of programme management is – support the process of involving the local community, agreeing priorities and appraising and delivering projects, but be prepared to keep your overall assessment separate until the time comes to share your conclusions. Don't over-manage the process, or give people who are not bound to you through line management the opportunity to cause delays by digging their heels in! And as ever, it's much easier to direct a programme if everyone involved has taken part in every stage of its development, and agreed all the steps along the way – build your team, work with your partners.

Performance Management

This is becoming a common buzz-phrase, particularly with delivery-focused organisations, and you may come across it if you are managing a regeneration team. There are two main aspects:

- What are the tasks needed to achieve your objectives?

- How well are your colleagues/employees/contractors/volunteers able to carry out these tasks?

Managing both of these things will be easier when there is a direct connection between the two, e.g. some training for a team member to help them carry out a particular task or function. A project plan will help you chart the first (see Project Management in Chapter 11) and regular supervision will help you manage the second. And of course, people will perform better if they can see you carrying out *your* functions well and achieving *your* objectives – be a good example.

Financial Management

Every accounting system is different – and you can double that for computerised systems – it's a fact.

Whichever system is inflicted on you, hang on to income and expenditure and you won't go wrong. We can all add and subtract (all right then, get a calculator), and the objective of course is always to have more money coming in than going out ... Keep hard copies of grant letters and the like (money coming in) and invoices (bills – money going out) and you'll survive – oh, and treat auditors as your friends, ask their advice, they'll be pleased!

Income and expenditure is also the basis of business planning, by the way. Once you have the bones of what the business or project is about, make the best-informed projection of income and expenditure over the first three years, and always leave some fat ('contingency funds') in case the projections are wrong – say, budget for costs 10% more than you expect, making sure income covers 110% of expenditure as a minimum.

Cash flow? If some months are going to be more costly than others, plan to have the cash in hand to cover that.

Risks analysis? List all the many things that *might* upset your projections and work out how to prevent them, or how to deal with them if they happen.

Risk Management

When in casinos, don't bet more than you can afford to lose.

However, that's gambling. Risk isn't that thing your mother warned you about, risk is about being aware of obstacles that might get in the way of what you're trying to achieve, and then managing them. We all know it's dangerous to cross the road, for example, but look both ways before you do, and you'll live. (My mother taught me that, too!)

But playing it too safe can be dangerous in regeneration terms, partly because if you don't make any effort then things won't change, and partly because regeneration is about change anyway, so an element of risk – things that might get in the way of change – is inevitable.

There are financial risks, of course, perhaps the first thing we think of (where's the money going to come from, will this project pay its way when completed?), but also physical, legal, political (with both a large and a small 'p') and community risks. You will find various model breakdowns along these lines, but the risk management approach is the same:

- How important is this risk?

- What can we do to prevent it happening, or to reduce its effect if it does happen?

A common approach to scoring risks is to measure:

- The chances of it happening, on a scale of 1 to 4

- The impact on your project if it did happen – top score of 4 for complete disaster, 1 if only a flea-bite

Then multiply these numbers together, so if something is bound to happen and would completely stop your project in its tracks – a top score of 16 – then unless you can head it off in some way, or take a different approach to your objective, the project isn't going to get off the ground (and shouldn't be allowed to!). A score of 0, by the way, for either impact or likelihood means it isn't a risk, so you should ignore it.

Aha, you say, but what if we ignore something from the outset and it later turns out to be more important than we thought? You should have a clear risk register for every part of your regeneration programme and review it at regular intervals – say monthly, or at programme steering group meetings. Keep your scores up to date, and keep a close watch on the actions needed to deal with the risks you've spotted.

(Incidentally, a hazard is not the same as a risk – a risk is more about the chances and impact of something happening, a hazard is the thing itself, like fast cars on that road you were crossing ...)

Policy

This is meant to be a practical book, but you will run into wider governmental or political policies eventually, probably by agreeing with one or violently disagreeing with it!

As well as informing practice, policies should also be based on practice. This means as you get more into the groove of regeneration, once again, your views will be as good as anyone's, so do get into the policy debates.

When planning your regeneration programme, you can find local, national and even international policies may help or hinder you. As ever, try not to be prejudiced in advance, as what is really important is your local regeneration objectives not the basis of views from outside the area – and policies can lead to funding.

> Rampant political ideologies can be a luxury. For many years I thought that once public funds became so short that all the political solutions were the same, rampant political ideologies might disappear. However, they have resurfaced as we go below comfortable budget levels, and are being used to inform the cuts being made in public funding and services. Silly me.

Get interested particularly in policies that may affect your opportunities, which can include planning policies but also priorities by which your local council spends or gathers its money. Selected local politicians of whichever political party can give you the background to the status quo, and you may find it necessary to deal with people whose overall philosophy you don't agree with in order to gain the support your regeneration programme needs. And if you come to a complete impasse, there is always the option of action to change policy (see Campaigning in Chapter 5).

Capacity Building

Regeneration is a long-term process. In order to make sure it continues after you've left the area ('exit strategy', or 'succession strategy' is better), start thinking now about the skills and perspectives local people, including businesses and local government officers, could usefully share and develop.

A good way to start is by attending regional or national conferences about regeneration. Take some local people with you to discuss what is presented in the light of your own place or neighbourhood, and this should be a useful springboard for more local action, as well as seeding the idea of excellence in what you're doing together.

Not everyone will want to take on everything at once, so think about a capacity-building programme around different perspectives and skills (see the contents pages of this book), and perhaps using open public meetings to bring more people in, as who knows how many will be required over time.

Be wary of being too pedantic about it all, but do quietly keep it going, as there's nothing worse than raising interest and expectations and then failing to support them. Aim for a programme that people sign up to and keep going after you've left, in parallel with the regeneration work itself.

The other reason for capacity building is that sometimes people will get into a leadership position and then block wider thinking by only following their own way. Danger. To be avoided. Rotating chairs are a good sign, not least for community groups. You will meet a lot of goodwill when you start a regeneration programme, but the more people that become involved, the more you are likely to find narrow views. Keep the debate alive, and above all, find and cherish your successors.

Learning

Even a seminar on your specialist subject will teach you at least one new thing – bound to, in fact. Learning about regeneration also makes a good break from working at whatever you're trying to do, so treat 'continuous professional development' seriously; you'll be better for it in more ways than one.

Then what about teaching other people? We know that:

- Some people grasp ideas easily

- Some people need to see a diagram

- Some people need to see things in reality

- Some people can be shown things, others need to find out for themselves

There is an 'experiential learning cycle' identified by David Kolb in the early 1980s (see Figure 9.1). Part of the cycle is about the process of taking in information (concrete experience, abstract conceptualisation) and part about how individuals interpret and act on that information (reflective observation, active experimentation).

To my mind, this encapsulates the different ways people learn, some by experience, some by reflecting on experience, some by fitting things into a logical pattern, and some by testing different ideas. Kolb's work has formed the basis for a wide range of other approaches, including one by Peter Honey and Alan Mumford who looked at the kind of people who preferred different learning styles – for example an activist can be seen (in my own words) as

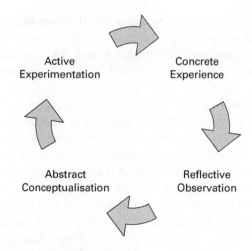

Figure 9.1   Kolb's experiential learning cycle

Adapted from Kolb, David A., *Experiential Learning: Experience as the Source of Learning and Development*, 2nd Ed., © 2015. Reprinted by permission of Pearson Education, Inc., New York, New York.

someone who prefers to go straight into trying something out without too much analysis in advance (and we all know people like that!).

There are personal tests that can be applied to help determine how individual people prefer to learn, but you may find that people are quite happy to discuss with you their own preferences and inclinations. Some people will pick things up well by being thrown in at the deep end, others feel the need to know more in advance. Ideally of course, we all learn best by going through the whole learning cycle as shown in Figure 9.1, as all the stages reinforce learning; so plan some reading and some thinking and some doing and some feedback when preparing training.

360 Degree Feedback

This is a team or staff management technique whereby managers invite their staff as well as their own bosses to give them feedback on how they're doing.

As a regeneration worker, your 360 degree view should include the community and local businesses you are aiming to support as well as your partners and steering group members. Don't forget, they can and should be the source of ideas and information as well as criticism.

Sir Christopher Wren is buried in the crypt of St Paul's Cathedral, which he was principally responsible for rebuilding following the Great Fire of London in 1666. His epitaph includes the phrase 'LECTOR SI MONUMEN TUM REQUIRIS CIRCUMSPICE' – 'Reader, if you seek his monument, look around you'.

Keep looking around you and checking other people's views if you want there to be a monument at all.

Celebration

We know things go wrong in regeneration, as in life, but for heaven's sake let's enjoy the things that go well!

Having a celebratory event or award is also a way of saying 'Thank You' to the many people who have been involved, particularly volunteers or other people who have given of their time freely. And don't forget to publicise the occasion, so that everyone knows what has gone well, and maybe some more people get excited about what you're all doing.

Funding the fun – how about getting local sponsorship of the event, that is paid back by the publicity? Party party par-tay!

Case Study: Llanelli Rural Council, Capacity Building

There are times when the world around you has changed, or you want to take it in a new direction, and you have to upskill yourself and your team for the task.

This example comes from Wales, where the Wellbeing of Future Generations (Wales) Act 2015 requires public bodies to work towards achieving seven national wellbeing goals:

1. A prosperous Wales

2. A resilient Wales

3. A healthier Wales

4. A more equal Wales

5. A Wales of cohesive communities

6. A Wales of vibrant culture and thriving Welsh language

7. A globally responsible Wales

This sounds like a familiar list for a regeneration worker! Public bodies working towards these goals are given advice about how to act 'in accordance with the sustainable development principle' by adopting five ways of working:

1. Balancing short-term needs with safeguarding the ability to meet long-term needs

2. Taking an integrated approach, by considering how wellbeing objectives may impact not only upon the wellbeing goals but also upon each other (and upon other public bodies' objectives)

3. Involving other persons with an interest in achieving the wellbeing goals and ensuring those persons reflect the diversity of the local population

(Continued)

(Continued)

4. Acting in collaboration with other persons to assist in meeting wellbeing objectives

5. Deploying resources to prevent problems occurring or getting worse, to help to meet wellbeing objectives.

Larger community councils in Wales (the equivalent of parish councils in England) are required by the Act to report regularly as to how they are performing against the seven goals. A number of workshops were held which community councils were invited to attend, after which the Welsh Government issued clear statutory guidance to help councils carry out their new responsibilities.

Mark Galbraith, the clerk at Llanelli Rural Council, reports that following good attendance at the relevant workshop the council have responded to what is effectively a requirement to work more collaboratively both internally and with the community and other external bodies in a number of ways:

*   A series of workshops have been held with the local community to establish and understand the main local issues (these have provided the extra benefit of course of upskilling and informing local people as well as councillors and council staff)

*   Views have also been gathered through online surveys

*   Discussions have been held with the larger local employers

*   This information has been gathered along with the latest available statistics for the area into the Llanelli Rural Area Whole Place Plan 2015–2030, which is now a resource to support local action in the future

*   The community council have also produced their own sustainable development policy to match the national policy

By adopting the five ways of working, the council report they have positively changed the way they work with the community. A recent example of this came when in deciding upon a new play area in one of the local ward areas, the council worked with the local school. The feedback from two community consultations held at the school and the input from the school council (made up of pupils that represent each year and sub group within the school) informed the council's actions in a way which in the past would not have happened. The resulting play scheme (selected by the school) reflects the needs identified within the community.

Above all in terms of capacity building, the council has employed a community development officer to help with the delivery of their Whole Place Plan. The council's formal reporting method has also been changed to include the five ways of working while demonstrating how the plan meets the seven national wellbeing goals. Darren Rees the community development

Opening of the new Pwll Play Area in November 2016

officer reports that this approach has been recognised nationally by Sustain Wales, the leading body for Sustainable Development in Wales, who short-listed Llanelli Rural Council for their Sustain Wales 2016 Awards under their Sustainable Public Service category.

Further Reading

UK Government (2003) *Managing Successful Programmes*. London: HMSO – the structured approach recommended to the British Civil Service, probably best looked at as part of a training course.

Honey, Peter and Mumford, Alan (1982) *Manual of Learning Styles*. London: Peter Honey Publications.

10
Financial Support

Money, money, money! Where can we find the financial support for our plans?

Fundraising

Money can't find people, but people can find money. The thing is – which people? It's hard work, and needs people with some time.

You will need clarity about three things:

1. How much money do you need?

2. Why – what necessity will you spend it on?

3. What will be the benefits or results from spending the money?

This basic information will help you to raise funds from a whole range of funding sources, and it will be helpful to review them all from the outset to make sure you're taking the best route to your objective, so consider:

- Grant sources

- Private investors

- Loans of different kinds

- Community shares

- Crowdfunding

- Payroll giving

- Support 'in kind' instead of money

- Government tax schemes

- Planning gain and other support from developers

The more community-focused sources are also an opportunity to spread the word about what you are planning, and some simple things like a modest fundraising event or a raffle (I won't try to list them all) can do more for longer-term local support and future funding than the amounts actually raised at the time.

This review of funding sources can also be an opportunity to look at your proposals as if through other people's eyes, and you may find there are wider connections or implications from your initial plans that may enhance your regeneration programme as well as opening up new avenues of finance. However, there is a danger of chasing after a source of funding because it's there, and in meeting the funders' requirements for what they want to support, you shift focus from what you are really about – so keep your core objectives in mind.

But all this takes time, which means you need enthusiasm! Either someone who is fired up and dedicated to raising money for your project, or hire a professional, but you must find that person from the outset or it'll take forever.

Business Planning

A business plan is essentially a set of income and expenditure projections for your proposal, backed up by some text explaining why you have made certain decisions and taken the described direction, and why you think the proposal will sustain itself in the future. It also classically includes a development time-table and an assessment of the risks.

Most if not all sources of larger funds will ask for a business plan for your proposal. The more experienced sources will be able to tell whether it is just a collection of facts put together to please them, or a real business plan which you are intending to put into operation. For the best results – and a useful exercise with your steering group, come to that – treat the document as a real route map for your project, and get everyone involved in discussing and agreeing the detail, so they 'own' the plan.

I have included a blank business plan template in Appendix 5, which I have used for building-based projects, and which hopefully gives you a steer on the kinds of thing to cover, but the original sin is a proposal that never covers its own costs and has to be bailed out or left to fail. In this case, the business plan exercise is telling you to think again!

As you might imagine, financial projections that go too far into the future tend to become increasingly fictional, not based on any reality. When you get to the financial section in the template you'll see it covers five years as some funders will ask for this, but honestly, anything over three years' projections is largely guesswork. Try to get some actual figures from somewhere as a reasonable benchmark and call it Year 1, and don't forget to allow for inflationary increases in future years.

As Mr Micawber says in Charles Dickens' *David Copperfield* (1849):

> Annual income twenty pounds, annual expenditure nineteen pounds nineteen and six, result happiness. Annual income twenty pounds, annual expenditure twenty pounds ought and six, result misery.

Grants

In a simple world, you can find a single organisation or funding source willing to give you 100% of the money you need in the form of a grant, provided you fill in the right application form.

Be prepared however to be speaking to more than one source, from the wide range available, which are fairly easily researched through your local library or with advice:

- Public funds – local, regional or central government grants for particular purposes

- Private funds – either sponsorship from businesses out of their own marketing budget, i.e. their logo on your project, or grants from larger firms that fund community projects

- Voluntary sector – many national and some local charities exist to give money to suitable ventures

You'll find there are different grant sources for capital money (one-off payments for things) and revenue money (cash to keep things going, less easily found). Grant givers of all kinds will want you to distinguish between the two, and will generally be happier to give short-term revenue money to something that will thereafter fund itself, rather than fund something that needs supplies of cash for ever. This means that a full business plan is likely to be an important part of grant applications, particularly for larger sums.

Whichever grant-giving body you're going to, give them a quick telephone call to be sure they are interested in your proposal – by and large, they will be willing to speak to you as they generally don't want anyone's time wasted on applications that are going to be dismissed out of hand. And when you do write in, make sure you use the same language they do when describing their grant scheme – if it's for community facilities in a preferred geographical area for example, use their descriptive terms when making it clear that your proposal fits their requirements.

Of course, if you're applying to more than one source for the same proposal – quite likely, as many grant givers will only give a percentage of your total requirements – you'd best make sure that you don't perjure yourself by describing your plans in completely different terms to each source ... This may cause problems later on, not least when issuing public press releases that all your supporters will read!

Investment

Applying for grants is time-consuming but relatively straightforward. However, sometimes there are opportunities for a more commercial arrangement with a source of private money – they give you money, but they get something back for their investment.

We're talking about other people's money here, so imagine what your own reaction would be if it was *your* money at stake?

People and organisations alike will be looking for a number of things in return for investing in your local regeneration scheme:

1. Some connection to their own interests or areas of expertise, be it commercial development or services to the community – or something new, if that's their fancy

2. Some financial return on their investment (otherwise, it's a grant)

3. There may also be a third, more topical element around financial markets, tax burdens and the like, including support for other areas of the investor's activity

Above all, investors will want to know how the rest of your regeneration programme will support their investment. They will like to see somebody else at the table to help share the risk – hence the importance of seeking match funding from different sources. Perception is very important – if people don't see how they can make money but instead see a load of grief, they won't invest (nor would you!). You need to be able to offer solutions to their concerns.

This is a specialist area, so as well as looking around at similar schemes, you will need advice on potential investors and where you might find them. There will also be preferred ways of stating your case, and even regulations to be aware of, such as those for major public schemes for countries in the European Union ('OJEU' regulations – all contracts from the public sector above a certain figure must be published in the Official Journal of the European Union), as well as contracts to be drawn up.

There used to be a published directory to potential private investors, but in this electronic age there are websites that may help, such as that of the UK Business Angels Association.

Browsing through this I came across London-based ClearlySo, an impact investment bank that specialises in making connections between private investors and businesses and funds that deliver positive social, ethical and/or environmental impact as well as financial return. One of their clients was the Green Rooms, an art deco former office building in London's Wood Green now turned into 'the UK's first arts hotel', principally designed to offer affordable accommodation to artists visiting and working in the capital but also playing an integral part in the regeneration of the local community and offering training opportunities for local people.

Rod Schwartz, the chief executive of ClearlySo, said, 'Our angel investors simply loved this deal! It combines urban regeneration, training, arts & culture as well as employment in one magnificent project.' One of the investors confirmed the value of the connection by commenting, 'I am delighted to be a part of the first arts-led social enterprise hotel in the UK and the energy that surrounds it – it is a positive and tangible way to support the arts with much-needed, affordable accommodation in London and it enables me to align investment decisions with my personal values.'

(UK Business Angels Association, 2016)

You might expect to have different types of conversation in boom periods where capital is looking for opportunities, than in periods of slump when opportunities are looking for capital. There is a further sub-division between people with their own capital and those who are borrowing from the banks, which adds another layer to these conversations – sometimes your potential investor has a banker behind them who also needs to be satisfied.

Whatever the situation, do your research – get advice – and be prepared for a time-consuming process with a varying endpoint. And do try to get past any hype from middle-men or -women, who can be helpful in making introductions, but are not responsible for making investment decisions.

I know of one instance when experts were worried about getting investors interested in a run-down city centre, but when the first site went out for expressions of interest, there were no fewer than 13 bidders. This is some credit to the site's marketing, of course, but I always thought there would be people interested in cheap sites with opportunities for financial return.

Social Investment

As well as grants and private investors, there are a growing number of professional social investors and intermediaries that specialise in making debt and equity investments into voluntary and community organisations.

> One of the pioneers of this in the UK was Andrew Robinson, whom I first encountered when he was Head of Community Development Banking for the Royal Bank of Scotland. Originally from Canada, he gave a talk that described how, finding that community ventures were no worse at repaying loans than private commercial ventures, he had campaigned for finance to be made as easily available to community development groups and social enterprises as to businesses. He also said that the prime objective of such ventures was the relief of the poor – not language we were used to hearing from banking circles! – and there needed to be a conduit for philanthropic funds to help social enterprises achieve their aims, rather than just loans for those looking for private profit.

The UK Sustainable Investment and Finance Association, launched in 1991 (Andrew Robinson is a former chairman), now has a long membership list of organisations offering a range of financial services. From the website of one of them, Social Finance Ltd, comes this summary:

> We realised that there were deeper issues at hand than simply the availability of capital for voluntary and community organisations. Those who pay for social services are not the people who use them. This creates a tension for service providers between the interests of their funders and their users. The funding of services may undermine their effectiveness. Alongside short-termism and bureaucracy in the system, this makes for a fairly dysfunctional marketplace.
>
> With this insight, we began designing a number of financial and advisory services and products for social sector organisations. We looked for structures that would offer flexibility and long-term funding, and would encourage innovation to deliver maximum impact.
>
> (Social Finance Ltd, accessed 2017)

Clearly, in order to provide funding for social ventures, finance firms need to attract investors who provide the monies in the first instance. One key tool that has been developed is social impact bonds, whereby investors gain a return on their investment depending on the extent of 'positive social outcomes' that the funding produces – there is no guarantee of a return on the investment, so investors also have to be dedicated to social improvement.

In practice, this means that regeneration schemes that need funding don't have to go to high street banks, there are other options available from social sector organisations who are easily researched via the Internet.

Community Shares

Turning to individual members of your community, there are a growing number of ways they can become involved in funding your regeneration scheme personally. If your core organisation – or a project-delivering organisation – is a cooperative or community benefit society (see Community Structures in Chapter 5), the classic £1 for membership can be replaced by a higher community share offer.

The posh phrase for this is 'withdrawable capital' – people can buy shares, but of course they may also sell them. Interest on shares may be permitted, but of course, there can be no guarantees about the return on investment.

The good news is that there is a lot of guidance on community share offers available from a UK national body, the Community Shares Unit, launched in October 2012 and continuing as a joint initiative between Locality and Co-operatives UK with UK government funding. There is a handbook on their Community Shares website produced under the supervision of government financial and treasury organisations, and the website also provides links to specialist practitioners who can help ensure the quality and success of your share offer.

Social Investment Tax Relief

This is a tax break that has become available under the UK Finance Act 2014, and can be used to encourage people to take up community shares or make loans to social enterprises by offering them 30% tax relief on their investment.

As you might expect with something under the eye of HM Revenue & Customs, there are a lot of qualifying criteria, for example:

- The social enterprise needs to be in the legal form of a community interest company, a trust or a company with charitable status, or a community benefit society

- The organisation cannot have more than £15 million in gross assets immediately before the investment is made.

- The organisation cannot be controlled by another company

- There must be fewer than 500 employees

(HM Revenue & Customs, 2014)

There's much more detail than this available from the UK government website. Happily, there is also an introductory guide, *DIY Social Investment*, written by Matt Fountain (2016), which includes a case study of how he discovered and used this approach for his project the Freedom Bakery in Glasgow. Have a read to find out if this is something for your project too (see also the case study at the end of this chapter).

Crowdfunding

This is another relatively new mechanism, usually applied via websites, encouraging and enabling people to support a particular venture. As the name suggests, a large number of people providing even modest sums each can add up to a respectable total.

There are many established websites that provide a platform for your crowdfunding appeal to make connections with your target audience. As well as being clear about what you want the money for, you will also need to be clear whether you are looking for donations, whether you are offering some kind of financial return on investment, or simply some benefits that your regeneration programme can offer such as reduced rates for using new facilities. And you will need to think about returning the money should the terms under which you are asking for it are not met – as for example if you don't raise enough to cover the cost of the project in question.

Going public with a crowdfunding appeal is effectively part of a publicity campaign, and the response to your appeal can show the depth of public interest in what you are doing. There are decisions to be made about how long you want to run any particular appeal for, but as you will appreciate, it will be as well to not go for funding to the same group of people too many times.

Corporate Payroll Giving

This is a process whereby people in your area (and wider) can give contributions to your projects through their pay cheques.

There are three agencies in the UK accredited by HM Revenue & Customs to manage payroll giving schemes (and other firms that connect to them):

- Charities Trust
- Charitable Giving
- Charities Aid Foundation

These can come to an arrangement with a company whereby employee donations can be sent to the charity of the individual's choice directly from the company's payroll, and the donations are sent gross of income tax, so (at the current UK income tax rate) a £12 donation effectively only costs the donor £10. Promoting such an arrangement may be useful if as part of your regeneration programme you set up a community or charitable enterprise that will continue to provide a local service over a long period of time – and to a relatively large local population.

The paperwork has to be done by the local firm in question rather than by you, but you can make it easier for them by describing the process with the help of an adviser – members of the Association of Payroll Giving Organisations could be one place to start. And you may find it helpful to include this as one option within a longer-term relationship you promote between your regeneration programme and local firms.

Donations

Sometimes people or companies can simply give you money!

Don't knock it – and you can make the option quietly available via your regular publicity or marketing.

One thing to establish is the capacity to reclaim UK tax on any donation, a process called 'Gift Aid' which can increase the donation by 25% – you will need to provide the relevant declaration forms, the UK government website can help you with this.

People may also give you help 'in kind' of course, which can be anything from the gift of equipment to the loan of somebody's time to help with part of the programme.

And don't forget to say thank you to the donors!

Legacies

Long-established charities such as Age UK provide discrete opportunities for people to leave money to the charity after they die. This is only going to be a useful potential source for a longer-term community or regeneration programme, but I thought I'd mention it.

Assets

The most difficult type of funding to secure is revenue funding – classically, regular money to pay staff.

One way of securing the future of a regeneration worker post is to acquire a physical asset – commonly a building that can be converted into offices or workspaces – and ensure it is sufficiently large, well-appointed and cost-effective to let out to tenants and secure a financial surplus from which to pay staff and their running costs.

There is a lot of good practice in running buildings like this, and there will be other local benefits from the building itself, which of course you will confirm through business planning before going forward. Finding the right building and acquiring ownership (plus of course the right paying tenants) will take time and money in itself, but the prize is something that can keep your regeneration programme going in the longer term.

Business Improvement District

This is an approach, tried in various parts of the UK, which needs some partnership development. Essentially, businesses in an area agree to pay increased business rates into a pot that they then use collectively to make improvements in the area that will in turn benefit their businesses. It may not work everywhere, and may be more difficult to agree in areas where businesses are already in serious difficulties, but for example is a feature of part of the recent improvements to Birmingham city centre.

The process naturally involves a stage whereby local businesses are invited to discuss the pros and cons of the approach, what it might cost, and what results are expected. Someone with experience of Business Improvement Districts, or BIDs, is usually brought in to manage this stage, leading to a vote by local businesses as to whether they wish to go forward or not – clearly, everyone in the designated area should be involved for the improvement district to be set up successfully.

As ever, fuller details of the criteria and processes are available on the UK government website, along with some useful case studies. Business Improvement Districts can be set up by the local authority, a business rate payer, a local landowner or a specific body set up to develop the BID, but in every case a proposal has to be developed and submitted to the local authority, along with a business plan. Should the proposal go forward it is the local authority that manages the voting process, but as a simple majority carries the day and all businesses in the area will have to pay the new levy regardless of how they voted, it's clearly important to get everyone onside from the beginning.

Tax Increment Financing

This has been tried in many places in the United States, and is if anything more controversial. The essential idea is that local government borrows funds to make improvements to 'blighted' urban areas, to be paid back when the anticipated improvements generate greater local taxes (tax increment). As you might imagine, this sounds great in theory, but apparently in some places has been misjudged and left local governments in financial difficulty. It's a regeneration tool to approach with care – a 'Newcastle–Gateshead Accelerated Development Zone' (same principle) was agreed with the British government in 2012, we await reports.

Public Works Loan

The Public Works Loan Board, part of HM Treasury, is established to make loans to local authorities in the UK and collect the repayments. This is an option available to parish and community councils in particular, where a capital loan can be repaid over time by raising the local parish precept (part of Council Tax – the rates) – obviously, you will want to ensure public support for this move!

Yes, there are official procedures. Yes, there are forms to fill in. The good news is that English parish councils are expected to take this approach with the help of their county associations and Welsh community councils with the Welsh government, so help and advice are at hand.

Planning Gain

This is a generic term for what developers can give to local communities in return for the privilege of – and in some cases, the actual permission for – building in their area. Sometimes this can be money or facilities given to the community direct, but most often planning gain is channelled through the local planning authority.

'Section 106 agreements' are the best-known mechanism in the UK for planning gain. The wording of UK Acts of Parliament is revisited over time, but you may be interested in the actual wording of Section 106 of the Town and Country Planning Act 1990 which currently starts off:

Planning obligations

(1) Any person interested in land in the area of a local planning authority may, by agreement or otherwise, enter into an obligation (referred to in this section and sections 106A and 106B as 'a planning obligation'), enforceable to the extent mentioned in subsection (3) –

a. restricting the development or use of the land in any specified way;

b. requiring specified operations or activities to be carried out in, on, under or over the land;

c. requiring the land to be used in any specified way; or

d. requiring a sum or sums to be paid to the authority (or, in a case where section 2E applies, to the Greater London Authority) on a specified date or dates or periodically.

(Town and Country Planning Act 1990)

Well there you go.

In practice, these obligations are negotiated between the developer and the planning authority as part of the process of granting planning permission. Of course, the developer can always claim poverty due to projected low profit from the development, and therefore an inability to make any contributions (particularly if it's a housing development, as there is a convention in the UK whereby the developer is allowed to make up to 20% minimum profit for themselves), but this is why these agreements are the product of negotiation!

Another approach available in the UK since 2010 is the Community Infrastructure Levy, which seeks to cut out negotiations and requires contributions for community benefit from developments over a certain size, to a fixed formula set by the local authority in advance. The Planning Act 2008 provides a wide definition of the infrastructure which can be funded by the levy, including roads and transport facilities, flood defences, schools and other educational facilities, medical facilities, sporting and recreational facilities, open spaces and affordable housing. This definition allows the levy to be used to fund a very broad range of facilities such as play areas, parks and green spaces, cultural facilities, district heating schemes and police stations and other community safety facilities.

> Local authorities are not obliged to adopt a Community Infrastructure Levy. Where I live, the two adjacent counties of Herefordshire and Gloucestershire have been waiting to know what the other is doing before rushing in, as they don't want developers choosing sites - and therefore counties - for new development depending on whether there is a fixed levy in place or not!

The best plan for a regeneration worker is to agree a list of what community facilities your area needs and make sure your local planning authority has a copy. Possession of a neighbourhood development plan increases the percentage of a Community Infrastructure Levy that a local authority must spend directly in the area of the development in question, but otherwise the sums raised through planning gain may be spent elsewhere by the local authority, so get your story in early.

Developers

As someone concerned with local regeneration, you must talk to prospective developers who want to build in your area.

In terms of finance, there may be benefits to negotiate in terms of planning gain, Section 106 agreements, Community Infrastructure Levy – in other words, monies that developers pay over in return for permission to carry out their plans. It will be important to get in early, and don't forget to make sure the local planning authority also know what support you are looking for. But there's a further prize as well in persuading developers to adjust their proposals where necessary to match your overall regeneration programme.

Anyone putting cash into a venture is entitled to a reasonable return on their investment, but this is not to say developers can't be reasonable about what they do, and there's more at stake here than profits.

We have seen in the UK a fairly standard development approach using well-known building firms – and familiar retail and housing tenants – that has proved financially successful in recent years as larger national organisations buy the local trade. The 2008 credit crunch has paused but not necessarily changed this approach – look at the 1980s and what followed.

(Some people seem to think we're still in the 1980s, by the way, despite the rule of untrammelled 'market forces' and sheer spending as a way out of recession being somewhat in question. Time for local self-sufficiency to be reconsidered, perhaps ...)

Any road, there needs to be an effective conversation with developers, involving architects, engineers, planners and local residents, otherwise all towns may end up looking the same again (remember the 1960s?), with only controversial design for variety.

How you have the conversation with developers is subject to local variation:

- Timing – either before or during planning discussions, or even after planning permission has been granted (but better early)

- Talkers – a range of people can get involved, from local government officers to community partnerships. Resident involvement in the Gloucester Quays development, for example, came about through a simple phone call from the chair of the local community partnership to the developer in question, offering links to local residents

- Teaming up – there may be financial benefits for everyone in bringing in other funding ('joint venture'), or even extending the site in question to include adjacent sites

See what can be done around local labour, local materials, local business tenants and local facilities. And there is absolutely no excuse for not talking with developers if the site in question is in public ownership.

And if you're in the happy position of marketing a site, you can research local needs in advance, and make them an integral part of the deal. This prevents the successful bidder saying 'Sorry, but that wasn't in the brief ...'

While I was writing this I thought, what will be the developer targets should oil shortages and climate change put a severe crimp in international distribution and exchange? What happens now in places where the global economy is not such a big factor?

In a more locally-based economy, perhaps we will move back towards what is perceived as the more medieval model of valuing the land, and people to work it – the means of production, in fact – with a side interest in more local distribution and exchange. I'm told the price of agricultural land in parts of the UK has doubled in recent years as farmers ponder the implications of climate change and invest accordingly. Perhaps supermarkets buying the trade in small towns are aiming for the best of both worlds, a monopoly of distribution centres both now and in the future, and not so daft, at that.

Case Study: The Freedom Bakery, Social Finance

The Freedom Bakery is a social enterprise that has established an artisan baking and catering facility at Her Majesty's Prison Low Moss (near Glasgow) to train offenders and enhance their employability. What started as an idea to help people coming out of prison and reduce reoffending is now expanding to a wider outcome, as there are now plans for a second bakery a mile from Glasgow city centre which will also provide employment opportunities for people as they leave prison – and there could be more such places across the country in future.

This is very much a people-based regeneration project, inspired by a similar scheme in Bologna in Italy, and set up by Matt Fountain who established the Freedom Bakery with two colleagues as a community interest company in April 2015. Following a feasibility study, the Scottish Prison Service gave the Freedom Bakery a four-year contract to establish a kitchen and cafe at Low Moss prison, but while revenue of at least £500,000 from bread and pastry sales over the contract period was projected to cover running costs, £65,000 was needed in the first instance to cover the set-up costs.

As the full total was not expected to be reached through grants, and as a community interest company limited by guarantee it was not possible to offer shares for sale, research was carried out to find social finance loan sources to cover the anticipated shortfall of £40,000. Unfortunately, of the three options identified, one was only available in Glasgow city centre itself, and the other two required borrowing a larger sum than could be comfortably repaid from projected income over the four-year period of the contract.

Following advice from the Community Interest Company Association, the Freedom Bakery took another approach, which was to set up their own loan offer, and aim to approach individual investors directly with the attraction of a guaranteed 30% return on investment through the Social Investment Tax Relief scheme. The detail of the proposal was a 7% return on the investment itself, with capital not repaid until the fourth year, and so the total cost to the bakery of borrowing the much-needed £40,000 would be £42,800 – a cheaper option than the other sources already considered.

This approach worked. The proposal document contained the example of a £12,500 personal loan to the project which would recoup £13,375 plus a further £3,750 in tax relief, in addition to the satisfaction of supporting the project's aims which would reduce the cost to the public purse of people reoffending. The offer was circulated through the project's personal networks, and raised the necessary £40,000 in a six-week period, and a further £8,500 in a second round a month after the first. A total of seven investors from Scotland to the South East of England invested between £2,000 and £11,000 each, one of whom redeployed their funds from an otherwise stagnant ISA (Individual Savings Account)! The majority of investors have said their main interest was in the project's social objectives, and it has become apparent that the 30% tax relief was of more interest than the 7% directly offered as a return on investment.

(Continued)

(Continued)

The Freedom Bakery at work

The project had a Plan B should this approach not have worked: a slightly more expensive strategy of going through an intermediary crowdfunding 'platform' (which charged a fee) to approach investors in a different way. A subsequent crowdfunding bid was launched to find £15,000 as part of the move towards a second bakery, and this reached its target in the last two days of the appeal following an approach by staff to the stars of the BBC *Bake Off* television programme! Never underestimate the power of connections ...

With the track record of repaying past loans, a sum of £250,000 towards 'Freedom 2' at the community-owned Rosemount Business Park has been raised from social investment provider Resilient Scotland, and the future is looking bright.

Further Reading

Hudson, Peter (ed.) (2000) *Managing Your Community Building: A Practical Handbook for People Running Buildings in Local Communities*. London: Community Matters (3rd edition edited by Jacki Reason) – a pretty comprehensive guide – downloadable from www.village-hall.org/files/Managing-your-community-building.pdf (Accessed 14 June 2017).

11
Projects

We're getting to the detail level now – how best to manage individual projects now we've started the overall regeneration programme.

Project Appraisal

Why should you or anyone take on a particular project idea? Appraisal is about asking some basic questions to prevent wasting everyone's time.

There is a pro forma in Appendix 6 as a checklist for this process, covering what the project is aiming to achieve, but key questions are:

- Is there a project leader or manager? Without anyone in charge, the best project in the world will not get off the ground.

- Is it sustainable – in particular, will it cover its annual running costs? If it's not going to continue to have an impact over time, it may be an indulgence to spend any money or energy on it.

- Does it have all the capital resources it needs, or is some fundraising required?

This last is not necessarily a killer, as we're talking about the start of a project not the finish, and if we have no regeneration funds at all, having a range of appraised projects waiting for their opportunity is not a bad plan. There are three outcomes from an appraisal – is the project a goer, is it no good, or do we need more information to make a decision?

Incidentally, project appraisal can work well in a group. It's a good way of getting people involved, and also spreading understanding about local issues. In Gloucester I had a pool of around 25 people I invited to regular appraisal sessions, and after a few meetings it didn't matter what people's background or expertise were, any half a dozen comfortably produced a full appraisal.

Project Management

This is about seeing things through, to time and to budget.

We all do this every day, in some way or another, but more complex projects need a more structured approach. There are many techniques, but Table 11.1 gives a simple stage-by-stage one by asking questions, in the steps of Rudyard Kipling:

> I keep six honest serving-men (They taught me all I knew);
> Their names are What and Why and When and How and Where and Who.

Source: *The Elephant's Child* by Rudyard
Kipling © 1902 Rudyard Kipling

The best book I've found so far on project management is the Dorling Kindersley publication listed in the Further Reading section, which doesn't use this exact approach but has very useful detail. There are some named

Table 11.1   Stage-by-stage guide to regeneration project management

WHY?	Be clear about the reasons for the project, as they will keep you focused and help you resolve any choices as you go forwards
FOR WHOM?	Who are the 'customers' for what you will produce? Probably not everyone! Whoever they are, include their needs in the planning, and get their comments before starting
WHAT?	This is the main focus of the project, what you will do and the expected outcomes. Some common types of project include: • New or renovated buildings, for work or housing • New community enterprises, say to deliver services • New or remodelled services, such as training • Environmental improvements, both green and urban • Marketing and promoting your area Make sure you identify 'SMART' outputs and outcomes (specific, measurable, achievable, realistic and time-related), e.g. which actual buildings renovated in what way with how much money from what sources by when

HOW?	Most of us rush straight into the 'how' without gathering the important clues above, which is dangerous as we may spend a lot of time and money on the wrong approach. Cost comes in here – can you afford the approach you are proposing, where will you get extra funds if needed, will fundraising itself take time?
WHEN?	This is about deadlines, when does the project need to be completed, and the timing for each stage. This is the context for your Project Plan, when you write down how you're going to carry out the work against a timetable. Cut the project into manageable stages (and plan to celebrate every one!). You should also look at risks to the project delivery which may delay it, or cost money to resolve, and review them regularly – don't assume things will always go just as you planned
WHERE?	This is not just about the location for your project (new buildings will need a site) or delivering services (how you will reach your customers, and the needs of distribution) but also where you will keep the necessary project records as you go along and where people can find out more about your progress. Depending on the length of the project, someone else may need to finish it, and various auditors will also want to look at the books as you go along – not to mention progress reports you may have to write yourself, and need to keep notes for
WHO?	Will you be the sole manager of this project, or are there others, and also a steering group of interested parties – 'stakeholders' who also want to see the project finished successfully and can help through regular contact?
WHAT HAPPENED?	Were your SMART objectives achieved? Did everything else go swimmingly, or are there lessons learnt you should share with others? Monitoring and evaluation is the posh phrase for this, and you need to start this from the beginning, which can also prevent 'project creep' – taking on more than you originally planned

methodologies, such as 'Prince 2', which has been adopted for use by the UK Government (2005).

If all else fails, I'm available to give my patent two-hour introductory course on project management.

Tendering

There is a lot of talk in this book about 'experts', and 'getting advice'. This is not always free! You will need to put some advice (and other work) out for local firms to 'tender' or bid for, hence the short-hand phrase 'tendering'.

You will need to describe the work clearly so people can tell you how much they will charge to do it. The resulting 'tender brief' for the work will contain a number of sections:

- Description of the work

- What it is intended to achieve – expected outputs and outcomes

- Expected experience and skills of the people who will do the work

- Timetable for the work – when you want it done

- Process for choosing the successful bidder. To prevent any arguments (see Naming of the Parts in Chapter 12), the criteria by which you will choose need to be clearly the same as the skills and experience described in the brief

As with most documents mentioned in this book, it is simplest to get hold of one from someone else and customise it rather than write your own from scratch – ask around – but meanwhile you will find a simple example in Appendix 7.

A lot of firms will ring up before the bidding deadline to ask if there is a budget for the work, so they can present their tender accordingly. Some people put a budget figure in the brief to save disappointments later, some don't so as to see how cheap the bids come in – it's up to you which way you want to play it. Whichever way you go, make sure again for reasons of fairness – you want to compare like with like, don't you? – that you give the same information to everyone, so you can compare value for money.

Some tendered work is straightforward, for other long-term work you may wish to interview people to get an idea of what they might be like to work with, and how they respond to new ideas (aha!). In those cases, get a couple of people to join you on a panel (normally including anyone paying for the work), first to select the interviewees ('shortlist') from the written bids, then to interview them. This will include listening to any presentations you may have asked for in advance about how they would do the work. You will want a score sheet for each member of the panel for each interviewee (and also for shortlisting – see sample in Appendix 8), listing all the criteria including value for money – cheapest is not always the best.

One last thing – and not everybody does this – I like to have an entry on the score sheet for 'ingredient x'. This is like unexpected star quality – sometimes people come up with something at interview that you hadn't appreciated, but which you suddenly realise will be very valuable for the work in hand.

And having chosen, make sure you have a clear contract that reiterates what is going to happen, when, to what standard, and linked to payments at each stage. It would be a shame to base a decision on value for money and then not get it ...

Value for Money

Some things are clearly not worth the price tag, others like health and education simply have to be paid for as the financial benefits are incalculable – but how do we deal with the things in between?

Value for money comes into its own as a practical discipline when you are comparing different options (and assuming you don't have endless money). The skill lies in creating a 'level playing field', a fair and accurate basis for assessing:

- The benefits of the various options

- The costs, ditto

- The ratio between the two

This is easier to do when you know what you are trying to achieve, as in tendering for a piece of work to be done. The worked example at Appendix 8 shows how you can score each benefit out of five and divide the result into the cost to give you a ratio as a basis for comparing different bids. Cheapest will not always be best, or most effective – make sure you have a minimum level of standards for meeting your needs, and be brave enough to turn down all the options if none of them is convincing or meets your budget.

Where it gets really interesting is where you could put funds into only one of three ventures, or use a piece of land for only one purpose, and there are different regeneration outcomes to choose from. How do you quantify different benefits for local people, where is your level playing field?

One example from my own area is the regeneration opportunity provided by the site of the last deep mine in the Forest of Dean, Northern United near Cinderford. Closed down in 1962, and only used for some dirty trades since, a wealth of local wildlife had colonised the area before a local councillor finally got the UK government to agree in the mid-1990s that, as an ex-mining area, the Forest of Dean and in particular the area of Northern United was eligible for some compensation funding.

It then took ages to reach agreement on what might be placed on the site, witness the fact that a brochure for potential investors and occupiers was only produced in 2012. Ideas around new workspaces and hotel/conference facilities developed into a relocation of the Forest's main college linked to housing development - long before which time local activists opposed to absolutely any impacts on the green environment of the Forest had swung into action.

I happened to be present at the District Council meeting when the regeneration plans were finally approved in 2013, and the only discussion at the meeting was around the impact on wildlife, with nothing about the other pros and cons of the regeneration options, as rightly or wrongly the campaigners had managed to totally polarise the debate.

So in such situations, I suggest you go back to basics, what you said you are trying to achieve (see First Steps, in Chapter 8), and then review priorities. Work up the options in some detail for comparison. People with a particular axe to grind will lobby for one outcome or another, but in those circumstances look more widely again – could their outcomes be met in another way? The best argument for a particular choice is if it is the only visible way to achieve one of the core objectives in your programme.

There are also mathematical 'cost/benefit analysis' techniques for addressing trickier comparisons, such as assessing complex services or processes to achieve a particular end, but we won't go there today.

Scale

Not every project works better if it's smaller. Some do, but some things only catch the wind and fly if they're larger – otherwise they won't work at all.

> One example is the plan we developed for a new neighbourhood resource centre in Gloucester. This needed a minimum of three paid staff to run it – one sick, one on holiday, one on duty – and it was easy to work out that there needed to be so much rental income to pay for these staff, which in turn set the ideal physical size for the building. This in turn put a higher target on the capital fundraising to build the centre, but the people concerned could justify it by saying anything less and the centre wouldn't pay for itself – a powerful argument with the local council!

So don't make everything bigger – have proper business planning in each case – but don't automatically drop the size either.

The Unexpected

So, you're all planned and ready, eh? Nothing can go wrong ...

Some organisations try to rehearse for emergencies, but nine times out of ten, what is missing from the rehearsal is the emergency itself, or at least the personal impact of it.

Failing to plan is planning to fail, but keep your wits about you when you start implementing your plans, keep your eyes open and keep your supporters close. Jungle ...

Case Study: Stag Community Arts Centre, Sevenoaks

This is an example of a project – and a site – that has been through several evolutions to get to its present success, ultimately with the support of the local town council.

The Stag was originally built as the Majestic Cinema, and opened in August 1936. The cinema enjoyed a golden era through the 1940s and

1950s, at one point providing one of the largest screens in the region, seating 1,360 people. In the early 1970s, the cinema was converted into a triple-screen complex, and plans were being made to include a disco.

But planning permission for the disco was refused, and a declining film industry and the arrival of home video meant that attendance numbers fell. Meanwhile the Sevenoaks Theatre Action Group (whose acronym has given the Stag its modern name) led by local thespian Margaret Durdant-Hollamby was campaigning for a much-needed theatre for the town. In August 1982, the campaign group received a call from the Rank Organisation which owned the cinema, offering the building for use as a theatre. Within 18 months the former cinema was transformed into a theatre, with a stage constructed without charge by a contractor who was building the nearby car park for a Waitrose supermarket.

The theatre opened in December 1983, but unfortunately the combined venue (two small cinema screens had been kept) did not survive financially. In a third approach to the building, the District Council acquired the Stag in 1992, and carried out a £3.2m refurbishment and extension creating the Stag Plaza, a self-contained venue used for drama, music, conferences and more. The revamped building was opened in December 1993, but struggled to cover its running costs, and closed again in 2008.

A formal bidding process then took place, which was won by Sevenoaks Town Council, who following a recent election had some new councillors and a very creative new town clerk. The Council spearheaded a proposal to re-invent the Stag as a Community Arts Centre, with a 25-year lease from Sevenoaks District Council from January 2009 – the District Council were also asked to provide five years of revenue funding. Town councils have powers to take on buildings and support community centres, but this was still a bold move (bearing in mind also the recession at the time) for a town of only 19,000 population and a venue that already had a chequered history. The business plan advocated using a 'hiring' model, letting out facilities and so ensuring that income could be known, and the use of 200 plus local volunteers, rather than being always dependent on ticket sales for survival.

The plan worked. A new company, Stag Community Arts Centre Ltd, was formed in December 2009, with the town council providing the registered offices and four councillors being the initial subscribers. The Stag became a charity in August 2010, and operates on a not-for-profit basis, reinvesting income directly into facilities in the Arts Centre. Events are run mainly by volunteers, but there is employment for around 40 local people (not all of them direct to the charity), and town councillors are still heavily involved. More detail can be gleaned from the annual reports submitted to Companies House, but there is a trading subsidiary, Stag Community Arts Centre Trading Ltd, which runs the commercial cinema side and gift aids its profits to the charity, which for the year ending 31 March 2016 came to just over £95,000.

Since 2009 a total investment of more than £550,000 has been put into the Stag by Sevenoaks Town Council and the charity, including replacement

(Continued)

(Continued)

The Stag Community Arts Centre – sometimes it pays to persist

theatre and cinema seats, 3D film projection, upgraded cinema projectors and cinema equipment, upgraded theatre lighting and sound equipment and refurbishing equipment throughout such as installing LED lighting and upgrading the Stag's 1991 mechanical and electrical (M&E) systems. The venue hosts an array of events and performances which appeal to audiences of all ages, and throughout its theatrical history has never missed a pantomime season! The Stag welcomes more than 25,000 people every month, more than 40,000 log on to the website each month, and extensive youth outreach work takes place every year.

This project seems to bring together so many things – local needs, local aspirations and campaigning, corporate assistance, intervention with the help of local councils, a new social enterprise, good business planning, but above all persistence – a long-term determination to keep and develop a venue for Sevenoaks that is for the benefit of local people and supported by local people. The Town Council commissioned an independent economic impact assessment which reported in January 2017, and states in summary:

- The Stag attracts around 250,000 to 300,000 visits per annum

- Total visitor spend is estimated at £9.2m per annum

- Some spend is captured by the Stag and supports 20 permanent full time equivalent (FTE) jobs at the venue.

- The remaining visitor spend, an estimated £7.6m, is captured in the wider local economy, supporting approximately 140 FTE jobs.

- The Stag is estimated to support a further 18 jobs through its purchasing power.

- In total, this equates to 179 FTE jobs supported by the Stag.

- After considering the effects of leakage, deadweight, displacement, substitution and multiplier effects, the total net impact of the Stag is 151 FTE jobs.

- This equates to approximately £7m of gross value added (GVA) contribution to the local economy.

- The Stag provides around 6,000 hours of volunteer opportunities for the people of Sevenoaks.

- The Stag adds cultural value to Sevenoaks as a place to live and visit.

(AECOM, 2017: 3)

Further Reading

Bruce, Andy and Langdon, Ken (2000) *Project Management.* London: Dorling Kindersley – I've not found the perfect book on project management, but this is my favourite.

12
Sustaining Yourself

You are the local regeneration worker – without your energy and stimulus, much of what you are working to achieve may not happen. So, look after yourself, and also watch yourself – how will you deal with the stresses along the way?

Health

Your own – look after it.

There are bound to be difficult situations and difficult people in regeneration, and you will need your own support group to bat ideas off, to have a moan with, and generally to keep you going. Spiritual refreshment, yes? If you have no manager, or are otherwise a solo worker, you will need to get this support from your peers or from outside work.

Also make sure you get enough exercise, and eat properly. If you find you're using alcohol, chocolate or other substances to relax, that's an amber light. Get advice.

'You should try and take things easier, Mr. Blue Arse'.

This may sound like mollycoddling (or even your mother!), but it's actually a professional responsibility – you're no good to anyone in a hospital bed.

Time Lord

Any of us could do a great job with unlimited time, but that's not on offer – we need to do what we can in the time available. 'The best is the enemy of the good', said Voltaire in 1603 – for example, better three projects completed with rough edges than nothing completed at all (he didn't say exactly that!).

One way out of this conundrum is to get help. When starting a new venture, think:

- Who could help me with this?

- Who should I tell about it? (Not necessarily the same people, but other stakeholders may have resources you don't know about)

Then look at the project 'timeline' – plan backwards from the project's end or objective to give you a clear idea when things need to be done by, what needs to be done before others can be completed, and estimate the length of time needed for each stage (this is called 'critical path analysis' – finding the most effective route to your goal). And monitor your progress.

Once you're working with other people, particularly on several projects at once, make sure you've given the others all they need to do their part before you get on with your solo work, otherwise you won't be ready to go forward together to the next stage.

And don't forget to say no when appropriate. One classic approach to a situation that keeps giving you work is to say 'OK, fine, I'll do it – but which other job would you like me to drop?' (And say it in a positive and constructive way, of course!) Keep a healthy view of what you can practically achieve through your own resources.

Also keep some development time for yourself (see Learning back in Chapter 9) – one hand for yourself and one for the ship, old sailors used to say. And add 10% of your time for publicity, for informing and involving others.

Sounds like you should plan your time carefully! That sounds reasonable (and professional) to me. Also, keep a note of how you spend your time, both for your own information and as a shield against uninformed criticism.

All right then, what about quality you say, if we're looking at three roughly-finished projects? Well, if you're setting realistic deadlines from the outset and keeping a close watch on progress – and have quality standards as part of the original project appraisal – then the results *will* be good, won't they? Just try not to get fixated and spend time on only one part of your work so as to create an artificial crisis, having to set unnecessary priorities, and carry out rush jobs to complete the whole thing.

Final lesson – for heaven's sake tell people when you're getting into difficulty with time, don't just plough on regardless, that's much more likely to end in tears.

Losing Your Temper

You're allowed to do this once.

Better? Now then, what got past your defences – was it a real issue, or were you just tired? Or both?

There are times when it's appropriate to lose your temper – some things are important, and some people (regretfully) only respect others when they stand up to them. So have the capacity to be tough by all means – don't intimidate without cause – but also take time out and look after your health, so that your enthusiasm doesn't trip you up unawares when you're short of sleep. Be assertive, not aggressive.

Or else!

And if you're writing an angry email, for heaven's sake sleep on it, and show it to someone you trust before you send it. An email goes round the world.

Naming of the Parts

Be honest.

Ultimately, it doesn't matter what you do (providing it's legal!), so long as you are clear about it, tell it like it is, and don't pretend it's something different when talking to different people.

Put another way – if you're wanting to pull something off for personal credit, it had better work for everyone else as well, or else it had better get you somewhere where those same people don't have to trust you any more (and where you will still have to live with yourself).

Selah.

Unpopularity

There will be times when you think, doing this will really make me unpopular. That's when you review the importance of your mission.

Try asking yourself, is what I'm thinking of doing vital to achieving the regeneration objectives? If so, you must simply go for it in a straightforward manner – you will actually gain more respect as someone who sticks to their goals, rather than someone who avoids difficult jobs.

And regeneration isn't about your popularity, is it? (No, it ain't!)

On the other hand, if being unpopular is going to make it more difficult to do the rest of your task, then get advice and find another way to achieve your objective. There are many UK regeneration organisations now (see list at the end of the book), so even if you don't have a mentor nearby, ask around for people who have faced similar problems before.

Saying 'NO'

Very necessary at times, otherwise you'll do too much and end up not being able to see the wood for the trees – or in hospital (see Health above).

An exercise – try sorting your in-tray into three piles:

1. Things that directly affect your (regeneration) objectives

2. Things that may be of professional or learning interest to yourself or to colleagues (pass them on)

3. Everything else – bin

Or is it actually saying the 'No' that's the problem? Try preparing different speeches – assertive not aggressive – standard reasons why you can't take something else on:

- Sorry I'm up to my eyes at the moment

- How about asking so-and-so?

- I'd love to, but not just now

If you *are* going to put yourself out for someone, be sure they will reciprocate at some suitable but early date. Mutual help is a particularly good mode for people in large organisations or partnerships.

Your Final Word

You can't touch tar and not be mucked – old English proverb.
You can't touch change and not be changed – you'll be different too.
So what do you think regeneration will change for you personally?

Case Study: An Inspiring Role Model

I wish to speak of Paddy Doherty.
  I knew him in the early days of the founding of the Development Trusts Association, now called Locality. To be an inspirational figure in the creation of a vital national organisation supporting local regeneration was a natural move for someone who was already doing so much for his home city of Londonderry (usually just called 'Derry') in Northern Ireland.
  When I first met Paddy in 1992 or 1993 he was in his mid-sixties, but still full of enormous energy and drive to help his community. I'm told he had originally come to prominence in the 1960s, when he was a founding member of Derry Credit Union. Also in the early 1960s, he was a founding member of the North West Housing Association.

(Continued)

(Continued)

The *Londonderry Sentinel* reports that as Londonderry became embroiled in the growing conflict, the city centre became a bombed out mass of derelict sites. In the early 1970s the vision of Paddy Doherty helped establish a group known as the North West Centre for Learning and Development. Its main aim was to try to tackle at base level the perennial long-term unemployment rate within the city. The first project undertaken by the group was the Old Foyle College Building, which was refurbished by Derry Youth & Community Workshop and became the Foyle Arts Centre. It is now part of the University of Ulster at Magee and houses the Performing Arts Department. The North West Centre for Learning and Development soon became the Inner City Trust and attracted support from across the community. From these beginnings and making use of government funding the Inner City Trust was soon involved in the redevelopment of a range of bombed out sites in the city centre.

Following the initial presence in London Street where its first project was Will Warren House, the Trust moved to work on sites in Shipquay Street, Bishop Street and Society Street and began on refurbishment projects there too. It is estimated that at one point over 300 people were working for the Trust on construction projects.

It wasn't all plain sailing. I well remember Paddy giving a presentation including a photo of the Heritage Library in Londonderry which had been burned down during the Troubles – and at the end of his talk he showed a picture of it since it had been rebuilt. He didn't give up.

The rebuilt Heritage Library in Londonderry

The scope of the project moved beyond the reconstruction of buildings in the city centre, and the Inner City Trust became involved in wider education projects. The Derry Youth and Community Workshop was established in 1978 and aimed to bring people back into the workforce by providing training in new skills as the traditional industries in the city began to disappear. The Workshop still operates as a training organisation, supporting and guiding the long-term unemployed towards and into employment.

Construction projects were not left to the side either, and in its most ambitious project up to that point the Inner City Trust built the O'Doherty Fort which is now the home of the Tower Museum. Next came the Craft Village, which remains one of most well recognised and attractive places within the city's walls. Other projects included the revamp of the Foyle Arts Centre on Lawrence Hill and a project on Rathlin Island. All the while the Trust did not employ the training school method of simply building something and then knocking it down again. The young people who mastered their trades there were able to take their skills directly onto construction sites.

If you stand at almost any given vantage point in the city centre today it is a fair bet you will be looking at something constructed by the Inner City Trust – the brainchild of Paddy 'Bogside' Doherty.

Paddy died peacefully in his home in Derry in January 2016 after a period of illness, in his 90th year. In his eulogy the Northern Irish politician Mark Durkan MP described him as a 'lion of civic ambition and community ethic' who had a huge pride in his city, its hinterland and its history, and an even bigger heart for its people:

> The whole city will join Paddy's family in their loss of a man of such warm inspiration and fond care.

> Paddy Doherty was a lion of civic ambition and community ethic. He was a true pioneer of methods of engagement and enablement which found wider practice with the development of the peace process.

> This was a man who could see problems but also recognised potential. His special ethic was to redress problems by releasing the potential, which was his working method in the Inner City Trust.

> He had dreams which he could turn into schemes, all driven by his ambition for the city and people he loved. He was a natural transformer who used change to enable more change. He could marshal his rightful indignation into purposeful initiative and recruit involvement to make things happen.

> He mixed a sense of mischief with achievement summed up in the adage that it is better to seek forgiveness than permission.

> Paddy liked to remind me that I had called him 'a prophet' many years ago. Today, as we witness how the City Walls are a shared

(Continued)

(Continued)

asset enjoyed by visitors, the renaissance of the Columba legacy, the vibrant renewal of heritage properties and cultural pulse in the Walled City, we should recognise that many of this prophet's hopes have been realised in his own city.

But he would also want to hear us urging for more so that the experiences of future generations could match his expectations for Derry and its citizens.

Helen Quigley, Chief Executive Officer of Inner City Trust, has said that over the last five years, the Trust has implemented a significant investment plan ranging from the creation of a new hotel, to the Shared Future Centre, the Garden of Reflection, a new Gallery Space to name but a few. The Trust continues to invest in skills development and has increased the 'Civic Dividend' – support for local charities which helps underpin the social fabric of the City. Mrs Quigley said that as the Trust goes from strength to strength, Paddy's legacy is being built upon and the dream endures.

If we need a role model to remind us what one person can achieve in regeneration, by working with other people to a common cause, we need look no further than Paddy Doherty.

Appendix 1 – English Indices of Deprivation

These indices were updated in 2015 by the Department of Communities and Local Government. There are 37 measures organised in seven 'domains', of which the income and employment domains are given greater weighting in the final scoring:

Income Deprivation Domain (22.5%)

- Adults and children in Income Support families

- Adults and children in income-based Jobseeker's Allowance families

- Adults and children in income-based Employment and Support Allowance families

- Adults and children in Pension Credit (Guarantee) families

- Adults and children in Child Tax Credit and Working Tax Credit families, below 60% median income not already counted

- Asylum seekers in England in receipt of subsistence support, accommodation support, or both

Employment Deprivation Domain (22.5%)

- Claimants of Jobseeker's Allowance, aged 18–59/64

- Claimants of Employment and Support Allowance, aged 18–59/64

- Claimants of Incapacity Benefit, aged 18–59/64

- Claimants of Severe Disablement Allowance, aged 18–59/64

- Claimants of Carer's Allowance, aged 18–59/64

Health Deprivation and Disability Domain (13.5%)

- Years of potential life lost

- Comparative illness and disability ratio

- Acute morbidity
- Mood and anxiety disorders

Education, Skills and Training Deprivation Domain (13.5%)

Sub Domain: Children and young people

- Key Stage 2 attainment: average points score
- Key Stage 4 attainment: average points score
- Secondary school absence
- Staying on in education post-16
- Entry to higher education

Sub Domain: Adult skills

- Adults with no or low qualifications, aged 25–59/64
- English language proficiency, aged 25–59/64

Crime Domain (9.3%)

- Recorded crime rates for: Violence; Burglary; Theft; Criminal damage

Barriers to Housing and Services Domain (9.3%)

Sub Domain: Geographical barriers

- Road distance to: post office; primary school; general store/supermarket; GP surgery

Sub Domain: Wider barriers

- Household overcrowding
- Homelessness
- Housing affordability

The Living Environment Deprivation Domain (9.3%)

Sub Domain: Indoors living environment

- Housing in poor condition
- Houses without central heating

Sub Domain: Outdoors living environment

- Air quality
- Road traffic accidents

(Smith et al., 2015: 18)

Appendix 2 – Matrix of Knowledge and Experience (English Agencies)

LEG: SECTOR:	PHYSICAL	ECONOMIC	SOCIAL
PUBLIC	Planning authorities, highway authorities, Homes & Community Agency (HCA)	Local Enterprise Partnerships (cover the whole of England), local council economic development departments (patchy)	Government departments, local councils
PRIVATE	Developers, housing associations	National and regional firms, colleges & universities	Health authorities, local doctors/general practitioners (GPs)
VOLUNTARY	National Trust, Campaign to Protect Rural England (CPRE), Community Land Trusts	Rotary Club, Chamber of Trade, Federation of Small Businesses (FSB)	Charities, voluntary action organisations, Locality, Action with Communities in Rural England (ACRE)
COMMUNITY	Local workers	Local firms	Local residents

Appendix 3 – Community Lexicon

Community action – a term for community-led initiatives commonly used in the 1990s

Community ambassador – someone appointed to represent local people at a regular group or meeting

Community anchor – organisation set up to support and develop local aspirations and help meet local needs

Community asset – property that returns an income to support community purposes (otherwise, it's a community liability!)

Community-based regeneration – regeneration as if people matter

Community building – the most common form of community asset, which hosts services and facilities for local people

Community cohesion – bit of a buzz-phrase, meaning people from all backgrounds living and working together harmoniously

Community college – organisation that supports learning where people are, rather than bringing them into formal education

Community consultation – this is what councils and developers often do instead of community involvement! Several techniques apply – exhibitions, questionnaires, focus groups

Community development – the process of supporting local people to improve their own lives, often through creating community organisations with particular objectives

Community development trust – generic name for a local organisation that seeks to lead local regeneration

Community engagement – generic term; when used precisely it means something between consultation and involvement!

Community enterprise – a social enterprise (see Chapter 6) that also meets a public need directly as part of its business

Community finance – generic term for community enterprises, credit unions (local banks owned and run by the savers) and any other way in which community-run benefit is regularly funded

Community forum – regular meeting of community representatives, often used as a basis for consultation

Community garden – does exactly what it says on the tin (and there'll probably be one – recycle it!)

Community infrastructure levy – new proposal from UK government for channelling 'planning gain' whereby developers pay money to offset the impact of their schemes

Community of interest – group of people with shared concerns, e.g. sports, not necessarily living in the same neighbourhood

Community interest company – new legal model for community enterprise developed by UK government

Community involvement – the best approach, bringing local people into regeneration projects from the outset

Community land trust – variation of a development trust focusing on housing, where the land is kept in public ownership to prevent future speculation that increases the cost of housing

Community leader – vague term used by the media for unelected community representatives! You'll know real community leaders by their actions and their following – and sometimes they are elected but not in the ballot-box way

Community learning champions – local people who meet other residents informally and make them aware of local learning opportunities – some also informal – and help them towards training and ultimately into employment

Community-led – any initiative controlled by a democratically-appointed community group who take care to reflect community need and demand in whatever they do

Community organisation – generic term for any group set up by the community to secure some public benefit

Community ownership – usually refers to something in the control of a community organisation, rather than legally owned by all local residents (as for example some charitable legacies)

Community partnership – a voluntary organisation of residents usually set up to work with other bodies to improve public services, e.g. with local councils over street cleaning (also called neighbourhood partnerships)

Community of place – residents of a neighbourhood

Community radio – community-owned and run broadcasting, usually featuring local news, views and businesses

Community regeneration – regeneration for the people, of the people, with the people!

Community representative – someone supposed to regularly bring local views to meetings and report back and forwards

Community safety – generic term for crime and disorder initiatives and concerns

Community shop – community-owned enterprise, becoming common in otherwise retail-free rural areas

Community space – weasel word for open areas in a development or housing estate, or even in a public building. Make sure it really meets community needs

Community transport – usually community-owned bus services, which have their own national association and standards, and which despite complexities around volunteers and insurance, can work very well

Community zero – any outspoken individual who thinks they (alone) appreciate every local view and know (without checking) everything that is required by the local community – or alternatively, the North Pole.

Appendix 4 – Expression of Interest in Workspace Pro Forma

Organisation

Contact name

Current address

Telephone

Fax

Email

Proposed activities

Space required (please give an estimated figure in square metres)

Office space

Storage space

Work space

Parking space (numbers)

Other (please specify)

Other requirements, e.g. special access, late hours, 3-phase electricity, anything that would affect the building design

Any constraints, e.g. budget, timescale

Any other comments or concerns

Signature & date

Please return the completed form to –
    Many thanks.

Appendix 5 – Draft Outline for a Business Plan

Contents:

Appendices:

Financial Projections

Appendix 5.1   Construction/Set-Up Costs (if appropriate)

Build Cost

Construction costs
Fees & services
Contingency
Design standards
Fit-out

Financed by

Grants
Loans
Partners
Total

Notes

Appendix 5.2   Income/Expenditure Summary

FIVE YEAR SUMMARY	Year 1	Year 2	Year 3	Year 4	Year 5	Total
Income						
Expenditure						
Surplus/(Deficit)						
Notes						

Appendix 5.3   Income Summary

FIVE YEAR SUMMARY	Year 1	Year 2	Year 3	Year 4	Year 5
Core users					
Other users					
Other income					
Total income					

Appendix 5.4 Expenditure Summary

Staffing Costs	No.	Salary £		Notes
Manager			On costs %	
Other staff by role			Pension %	
			Inflation %	

	Year 1	Year 2	Year 3	Year 4	Year 5
Salaries					
Employers' National Insurance					
Employers' Pension Costs					
Health Insurance					
Temporary staff/Redundancy					
Recruitment/Police Checks					
Staff Travel					
Staff Training					
Trustees and Volunteer Expenses					

Appendix 5.5 Expenditure Summary continued

	Year 1	Year 2	Year 3	Year 4	Year 5
Staff costs (total from above)					
Electricity & gas					
Telecommunications					
Water					
Postage					
Stationery					
Printing					
Supplies					
Food & drink					
Maintenance (fire/lift, etc.)					
Vehicle maintenance					
Vehicle running costs					
Vehicle fuel					
Cleaning					
Refuse					
Equipment leasing					
Equipment repair					
Audit & accountancy					
Legal fees					
Professional fees					
Depreciation					
TOTAL COSTS					
Notes					

Appendix 6 – Project Appraisal Format

Appendix 6.1

Project title

Project lead

Partners
(confirmed/not)

Project description, including any options, and proposed approach

Project history, including research & consultation to date

Need for the project

Scope/size of project

Location

Measurable outcomes/other benefits

Support for other strategies/objectives

Cost estimates
(capital/revenue)

Income sources (confirmed/not)

Sustainability

Risks

Assessment

Next steps

Appraiser & date

Appendix 6.2 Project Appraisal Guidance Notes

Project lead	Project champion/origin if no named lead
Partners (confirmed/not)	
Project description, including any options, and proposed approach	Enough information to inform a 'mandate' for the project to go forward, fuller details will be for the next, 'project initiation' stage (Prince 2 terms). Test if proposers have considered the zero option
Project history, including research & consultation to date	
Need for the project	Evidence base, e.g. indicators of deprivation, housing needs survey, other research
Scope/size of project	Range of activity, partners and beneficiaries. Physical size if capital project, area of operation/benefit if revenue project
Location	
Measurable outcomes/other benefits	Benefits for whom? Issues of exactly how to measure outcomes to be addressed at the next stage, project initiation
Support for other strategies/ objectives	• Crime & Disorder/Community Safety • Community Strategy • Cultural Strategy • Economic Development Strategy • Other local/regional/national
Cost estimates (capital/revenue)	
Income sources (confirmed/not)	Could be support in kind through staff time, etc.
Sustainability	Long-term prospects in environmental/economic/social terms
Risks	Risks that would prevent the project happening, and risks if the project doesn't happen (zero option)
Assessment	1. Project should go forward, seek resources 2. Project needs more research 3. Project should not go forward because … 4. Other comment
Next steps	From the appraisal meeting, not necessarily for the project itself

Appendix 7 – Sample Tender Brief

Newtown Regeneration Partnership

Brief for Resurfacing Town Hall Car Park

Newtown Town Council owns the Town Hall and adjacent car park in Newtown High Street. As part of the regeneration plans for the town, the Town Council have agreed with Newtown Regeneration Partnership the need to resurface the car park, with an eye to the implications of water drainage following recent flooding of the Town Hall.

Tasks

The work should be carried out in two phases:

1. Detailed plan of the work for approval before proceeding further, indicating precautions taken to manage surface water, which will include a 50mm slope away from the building to an edged kerb or surface drain, and care of the destination of that water in the event of excess rainfall or flood. There should also be consideration of the best place for disabled car parking, and for a turning circle at the bottom end of the car park

2. Work on site, including the following tasks:

    o   Scrape off the existing surface and remove arisings to tip

    o   Provide and lay drainage channels as required

    o   Provide and lay a new surface of appropriate sub-base material

The work will require skills in surveying and drafting as well as road engineering, drainage and site management, and should be completed as soon as possible.

Budget

There is currently a budget of up to £10,000 for this work. The Town Council would like to see the whole of the parking area resurfaced, down to the oil tank at the rear of the site, but are conscious that even if the resurfacing is not finished with tarmac, but some sub-base material becomes the preferred solution, the current budget may not take us that far.

Please could tender replies include a clear justification for any cost proposals.

Tenders

Bids for the completion of this work should please include the following:

- A proposal for how and when the work should be carried out, including the principal tasks in each phase

- Details of your staff's skills and previous experience with similar work

- An order of costs

- A suitable financial reference

- Confirmation of insurance cover

- Any comments on the brief itself

Selection process

Bids will be reviewed by a sub-committee of the Newtown Regeneration Partnership against the details requested above. Bidders may be asked to give a presentation at the next Town Council meeting from 7.30 pm on July 15th.

Deadline

All bids should be returned in a sealed envelope marked "TOWN HALL CAR PARK" by noon on 1st July to:

Newtown Regeneration Partnership

Town Hall

High Street

Newtown

AN1 PL5

Contact

Please contact the town clerk for any further information or to arrange a site visit – Many thanks.

Appendix 8 – Sample Tender Score Sheet

Score each item out of 5 (except those in italics)	SMITH & CO	JONES BROS.	ROBINSONS LTD
Detailed explanation of the proposed approach	4	3	3
Skills required (separate scoreline for each one)	5	3	4
Experience/track record (of staff, not firm)	3	3	3
Financial reference (bank, or recent accounts)	4	2	1
Ingredient 'x' (any extra talents not already noted)	3	0	1
Subtotal	*19*	*11*	*12*
Total cost (from tender)	*£12,000*	*£11,000*	*£10,000*
Cost divided by subtotal	*632*	*1,000*	*833*
Value for Money rating (lowest figure above is best)	3	1	2
TOTAL SCORE	**22**	**12**	**14**
Notes	Best value for money	Third choice	Runner-up

Bibliography

Action for Market Towns (2005) *Market Towns Healthcheck Handbook.* Bath.

AECOM Ltd (2017) *Economic Impact Assessment of The Stag Community Arts Centre.* Sevenoaks Town Council private report.

Batty, Elaine; Beatty, Christina; Foden, Mike; Lawless, Paul; Pearson, Sarah and Wilson, Ian (2010) *The New Deal for Communities Experience: A Final Assessment.* London: Department for Communities and Local Government – downloadable from http://extra.shu.ac.uk/ndc/downloads/general/A%20final%20assessment.pdf (Accessed 14 June 2017).

BRE Global Ltd (2014) *BREEAM UK: New Construction: Non-domestic Buildings (United Kingdom) Technical Manual.* Watford: BRE – downloadable from www.breeam.com/BREEAMUK2014SchemeDocument/ (Accessed 14 June 2017).

BRE Global Ltd (2015) *Home Quality Mark: Technical Manual.* Watford: BRE – downloadable from www.homequalitymark.com/filelibrary/HQM--December-2015-.pdf (Accessed 14 June 2017).

CEEQUAL Ltd (2015) *CEEQUAL Scheme Description for Projects and Term Contracts.* Watford: BRE – downloadable from www.ceequal.com/scheme-descriptions/ (Accessed 14 June 2017).

Clayden, Paul (2016) *Arnold-Baker on Local Council Administration*, 10th edition. London: LexisNexis.

Collins, Jim (2001) *Good to Great: Why Some Companies Make the Leap ... And Others Don't.* New York: Harper Business.

Campaign to Protect Rural England with the National Association of Local Councils (2012) *How to Shape Where You Live: A Guide to Neighbourhood Planning.* London – downloadable from www.cpre.org.uk/resources/housing-and-planning/planning/item/2689-how-to-shape-where-you-live-a-guide-to-neighbourhood-planning (Accessed 14 June 2017).

The Countryside Agency (2002) *Market Towns Health Check.* London.

The Countryside Agency (2004) *Parish Plans: Guidance for Parish and Town Councils.* London – downloadable from http://eastdevon.gov.uk/media/253289/guidance-to-parish-councils.pdf (Accessed 8 September 2017).

Department for Communities and Local Government (2012) *The National Planning Policy Framework* – downloadable from www.gov.uk/government/publications/national-planning-policy-framework--2 (Accessed 14 June 2017).

Department for Regional Development (2012) *Regional Development Strategy 2035.* Belfast – downloadable from www.infrastructure-ni.gov.uk/publications/regional-development-strategy-2035 (Accessed 14 June 2017).

Equal Lives – downloadable from www.equallives.org.uk (Accessed 6 March 2017).

Fountain, Matt (2016) *DIY Social Investment*. London: Big Society Capital and Flip Finance – downloadable from http://flipfinance.org.uk/2016/05/06/a-social-entrepreneurs-guide-to-social-investment-tax-relief-sitr/ (Accessed 14 June 2017).

Gloucester Heritage Urban Regeneration Company (2006) *Area Regeneration Framework*.

Hodgson, Jacqui with Hopkins, Rob (2010) *Transition in Action, Totnes and District 2030, an Energy Descent Action Plan*. Transition Town Totnes – downloadable from www.transitiontowntotnes.org/groups/building-and-housing/energy-descent-action-plan (Accessed 8 March 2017).

HM Government (2005) *Sustainable Communities: Homes for All*. London: Office of the Deputy Prime Minister – downloadable from http://webarchive.nationalarchives.gov.uk/20120919132719/http:/www.communities.gov.uk/documents/corporate/pdf/homes-for-all.pdf (Accessed 14 June 2017).

HM Revenue & Customs (2014) *Social Investment Tax Relief (SITR): Guide for Social Enterprises* – downloadable from www.gov.uk/government/uploads/system/uploads/attachment_data/file/378085/se-guide.pdf (Accessed 6 March 2017).

Hopkins, Rob (2008) *The Transition Handbook – From Oil Dependency to Local Resilience*. Totnes: Green Books.

The Intergovernmental Panel on Climate Change (2014) *Climate Change 2013 – The Physical Science Basis: Working Group I Contribution to the Fifth Assessment Report of the Intergovernmental Panel on Climate Change*. Cambridge: Cambridge University Press – downloadable from http://climatechange2013.org/ (Accessed 14 June 2017).

Joseph Rowntree Foundation (2016) *We Can Solve Poverty in the UK*. York – downloadable from www.jrf.org.uk/report/we-can-solve-poverty-uk (Accessed 14 June 2017).

Kolb, David (2015) *Experiential Learning: Experience as the Source of Learning and Development*. 2nd edition. New York: Pearson Education Inc.

McGregor, Douglas (1960) *The Human Side of Enterprise*. New York: McGraw-Hill.

Pawson, Hal; Fancy, C.; Morgan, James and Munro, M. (2005) *Learning the Lessons from the Estates Renewal Challenge Fund*. London: Office of the Deputy Prime Minister.

Review of the Register Report (1999) *Promotion of Urban and Rural Regeneration*. London: The Charity Commission – downloadable from www.gov.uk/government/publications/promotion-of-rural-and-urban-regeneration-rr2 (Accessed 14 June 2017).

Rhodes, John; Tyler, Peter; Brennan, Angela et al. (2007) *The Single Regeneration Budget: Final Evaluation*. Cambridge: Cambridge University – downloadable from www.landecon.cam.ac.uk/pdf-files/urban-and-regional-analysis/part1-final-eval-feb-07.pdf (Accessed 14 June 2017).

Scottish Government (2014a) *Ambition, Opportunity, Place – Scotland's Third National Planning Framework*. Edinburgh – downloadable from www.gov.scot/Publications/2014/06/3539/downloads (Accessed 14 June 2017).

Scottish Government (2014b) *Scottish Planning Policy*. Edinburgh – downloadable from www.gov.scot/Publications/2014/06/5823/downloads (Accessed 14 June 2017).

Secured by Design (2015) *Commercial Developments 2015*. London – downloadable from http://www.securedbydesign.com/wp-content/uploads/2015/05/SBD_Commercial_2015_V2.pdf (Accessed 9 August 2017).

Secured by Design (2016) *Homes 2016*. London – downloadable from http://www.securedbydesign.com/wp-content/uploads/2017/06/Secured_by_Design_Homes_2016_V2.pdf (Accessed 9 August 2017).

Skills Funding Agency (2016) *Apprenticeship Funding: Rules and Guidance for Employers*. London – downloadable from www.gov.uk/government/uploads/system/uploads/attachment_data/file/605004/EMPLOYER_RULES_V2_FINAL.pdf (Accessed 14 June 2017).

Smith, Tom; Noble, Michael; Noble, Stefan; Wright, Gemma; McLennan, David and Plunkett, Emma (2015) *The English Indices of Deprivation 2015: Technical Report*. London: Department for Communities and Local Government – downloadable from www.gov.uk/government/uploads/system/uploads/attachment_data/file/464485/English_Indices_of_Deprivation_2015_-_Technical-Report.pdf (Accessed 14 June 2017).

Social Finance Ltd – downloadable from www.socialfinance.org.uk/about-us/history (Accessed 8 March 2017).

Staunton Parish Council (2007) *Staunton Parish Plan 2007–2010*. Gloucestershire – downloadable from www.fdean.gov.uk/media/3823/staunton-corse-parish-pla.pdf (Accessed 14 June 2017).

Town and Country Planning Act 1990, s.106. – downloadable from www.legislation.gov.uk/ukpga/1990/8/section/106 (Accessed: 6 March 2017). Reprinted under the Open Government Licence 3.0. Available at: www.nationalarchives.gov.uk/doc/open-government-licence/version/3/.

Transition Network Team (2016) *The Essential Guide to Doing Transition – Your Guide to Starting Transition in Your Street, Community, Town or Organisation*. Transition Network – downloadable from www.transitionnetwork.org/resources/essential-guide-transition (Accessed 8 March 2017). Created by Rob Hopkins and Michael Thomas, with input from Sophy Banks, Ainslie Beattie, Ben Brangwyn, Naresh Giangrande, Sarah McAdam, Claire Milne, and Transitioners around the world.

UK Business Angels Association (2016) – downloadable from www.ukbusinessangelsassociation.org.uk/news/angels-back-green-rooms-arts-hotel-offer-affordable-rooms-urban-regeneration (Accessed 6 March 2017).

UK Government (2005) *Managing Successful Projects with Prince 2*. London: HMSO.

UNESCO (2001) *UNESCO Universal Declaration on Cultural Diversity*. Paris: UNESCO Publishing – downloadable from www.un-documents.net/udcd.htm (Accessed 14 June 2017).

Welsh Government (2008) *The Wales Spatial Plan – People, Places, Futures.* Cardiff – downloadable from gov.wales/topics/planning/development-plans/wales-spatial-plan/?lang=en (Accessed 14 June 2017).

Welsh Government (2016) *Planning Policy Wales.* 9th edition. Cardiff – downloadable from http://gov.wales/topics/planning/policy/ppw/?lang=en (Accessed 14 June 2017).

Wolf, Alison (2015) *Fixing a Broken Training System: The Case for an Apprenticeship Levy. A Report for the Social Market Foundation.* London – downloadable from www.smf.co.uk/wp-content/uploads/2015/07/Social-Market-Foundation-Publication-Alison-Wolf-Fixing-A-Broken-Training-System-The-Case-For-An-Apprenticeship-Levy.pdf (Accessed 14 June 2017).

World Commission on Environment and Development (1987) *Our Common Future.* Oxford and New York: Oxford University Press – key text in Chapter 2 downloadable from www.un-documents.net/ocf-02.htm (Accessed 6 March 2017).

Course Notes

If I were going to design a course on regeneration, I'd use the following themes that are reflected in this book's chapter headings. Each of the 12 is capable of infinite expansion, so it could be a 12-day course or 12 weeks. I have assumed the course is based in a regeneration area, so local examples can be used. I've also suggested some course work, site visits, topics for visiting lecturers, group exercises, and summarised learning points in the form of a test.

Introduction to Regeneration

Book sections	What's It All About?
	World View
	One-shot Solutions
	Outputs and Outcomes
	Sustainable Development
	Connections
	Experts
	Empowerment
	UK Regeneration Organisations
	Bibliography
Lecture	Regeneration examples from around the world
Site visit	Library/websites
Group exercise	Discuss expectations of regeneration
Course work	Sources of information on regeneration
Learning points	What is regeneration?
	How will we know we have succeeded?
	Who will be involved?
	Where can we get help and advice?

Why Regenerate?

Book sections	Poverty
	Cycles of Deprivation
	Sustainable Communities
	Community
	Community Cohesion
	Culture
Lecture	Community aspirations
Site visit	Poor and rich areas
Group exercise	Discuss common ground in regeneration
Course work	Plan for a local need and demand study
Learning points	What is the community?
	How can we identify their needs?
	How can they work together?
	Why is their involvement important?
	What do they bring to the process?

Local and Global Economies

Book sections	Mickey Marx Economics
	Business
	Social Enterprise
	Economic Development
	Training for Employment
Lecture	Local business organisations
Site visit	High street and industrial estate
Group exercise	Discuss local economic priorities
Course work	Map local routes to employment
Learning points	Who are the local businesses?
	Which are taking more than they give?
	How healthy is the local economy?
	What is clearly missing?
	What more can be done locally?
	Where should we look for outside help?

What You See Is What You Get

Book sections	Physical Regeneration
	Housing
	Workspace
	Public Realm
	Leisure
	Brownfield and Greenfield
	Archaeology
	Underground
	Design

Lecture	Local housing and workspace needs
Site visit	Different housing tenures
Group exercise	Discuss priorities for the built environment
Course work	Describe the local travel-to-work area
Learning points	How do we determine building needs? What are the key design issues? What are the obstacles to delivery? How do we assess priorities?

Cross-cutting Issues

Book sections	Environment Climate Change Renewable Energy Water Peak Oil Transport Diversity Population Planet Change
Lecture	Breadth of climate change impacts
Site visit	Key impact points, e.g. drains, road junctions
Group exercise	Discuss potential areas for crisis
Course work	'Future-proofing' local regeneration
Learning points	How do these issues impact on regeneration? How can we work with each one? Where do we go for potential solutions?

Team Work

Book sections	Partnership Working Joined-up Regeneration Sectors Publicity Influencing Negotiating Conflict Leadership People Management Fun Volunteers Policy
Lecture	Local politics
Site visit	Local government meeting
Group exercise	Discuss key players in local decisions
Course work	Local influencing plan
Learning points	Who are the (many) decision makers? How do we reach and involve them?

Planning

Book sections	First Steps
	SWOT Analysis
	Evidence Base
	Local Identity
	Land Use Planning
	Masterplanning
	Town Planning
	Fashion
	Innovation
	Transition Initiatives
Lecture	Local Development Framework (Local Plan)
Site visit	Derelict local areas
Group exercise	Discuss opportunities for regeneration
Course work	Local SWOT analysis
Learning points	What is the planning process?
	Who needs to be involved?
	How do we agree the way forward?
	Where is the key information?

Regeneration Management

Book sections	Programme Management
	Performance Management
	Financial Management
	Risk Management
	Capacity Building
	Learning
	Celebration
Lecture	Programme management
Site visit	Building site office
Group exercise	Risk assessment – identification and mitigation
Course work	Risk management strategy for the local programme
Learning points	What can go wrong?
	How can we prevent that?
	What skills are needed?
	What are the key factors to ensure success?

Development

Book sections	Fundraising
	Investment
	Developers
Lecture	A developer's perspective

Site visit	Prime or controversial development site
Group exercise	Discuss options for the development
Course work	Marketing plan for the local area
Learning points	How do investors view local areas? What influences their decisions? What obstacles do developers face? How can they be linked to local plans? Where else can funding be found?

Projects

Book sections	Project Appraisal Project Management Tendering Value for Money Scale
Lecture	Introduction to project management
Site visit	Newly-finished project(s)
Group exercise	Appraise some key local proposals
Course work	Programme of projects for local regeneration
Learning points	What are the skills of project development? What are the key criteria for success? How do we appraise potential projects? How do we manage them once started? How do we assess value for money?

Troubleshooting

Book sections	Great Expectations Eureka Moment Knee-jerk Reactions Understanding The Pits Clever Clogs Vanity Regeneration
Lecture	Human weaknesses
Site visit	Project that has gone wrong
Group exercise	How might the project have been saved?
Course work	Risk assessment of project proposals
Learning points	How can you plan for the impact of people? What are the warning signs to look out for? How do we assess others? What can we do about it? Will it always be worth the grief?

Personal Approach

Book sections	Health
	Time Lord
	Losing Your Temper
	Naming of the Parts
	Unpopularity
	Saying 'NO'
	Capacity Building
	Your Final Word
Lecture	Work planning
Site visit	Regeneration seminar or conference
Group exercise	Discuss how to sustain local regeneration
Course work	Personal development plan
Learning points	What are your personal strengths?
	What are your weaknesses?
	How do we gain a real perspective on ourselves?
	What do we do about what we find?
	How can we sustain a regeneration process?

Dissertation – A Local Regeneration Strategy

Final passing test – who are the local people who can help or advise you with every aspect of regeneration – highways, housing, commercial letting, community involvement and the rest – and what are their names and telephone numbers?

Don't forget that email – words alone – only carries 7% of human messages. The voice on the telephone carries 36% more clues, but people need to see your body language (and you to see theirs) for full communication. So meet them first, email them after.

Cultural References

There are several popular songs that speak to me of regeneration:

'Fan the Flames' – we gotta work together to make the most of this go-round (thank you John 'Juke' Logan).

'It Ain't Easy, Being Green' – Kermit the Frog should know.

'Let's Work Together' – Canned Heat said it.

'Mary Ellen Carter' – by Stan Rogers, the only folk song about the sinking ship where the ship comes back up again! Rise again ...

'Spread a Little Happiness' – by Vivian Ellis, Greatrex Newman and Clifford Grey – if it don't bring delight, it ain't right.

'Tain't What You Do It's The Way That You Do It' – by Sy Oliver and James Young – how true.

You'll think of more taglines that sing to you – we all need something to keep us going at times, or just a motto or picture to put on our desks.

And if you want a real metaphor of the individual working with strangers on a novel task to improve local facilities, seek out the film *Lilies of the Field* (1963) for which Sidney Poitier got his Oscar.

UK Regeneration Organisations

You can find a whole host of useful contacts by looking on the Internet, but here are some to start with:

ACRE – Action with Communities in Rural England

01285 653477 www.acre.org.uk

ATCM – Association of Town Centre Management – has published good practice, but individual membership is no longer available, only for town centre management schemes, with a new scheme for smaller towns

0207 222 0120 www.atcm.org

CLES – Centre for Local Economic Strategies – publishes good practice and organises training events

0161 236 7036 www.cles.org.uk

Co-operatives UK – the network for Britain's thousands of co-operative businesses

0161 214 1750 www.uk.coop

CPRE – Campaign to Protect Rural England – offers a wide range of guidance as well as campaigning

0207 981 2800 www.cpre.org.uk

CREW – Centre for Regeneration Excellence in Wales

01792 479293 www.regenwales.org

Development Trusts Association (DTA) Scotland – the national body for development trusts in Scotland

0131 220 2456 www.dtascot.org.uk

Development Trusts Association (DTA) Wales – the national body for development trusts in Wales

02920 190260 www.dtawales.org.uk

DSC – Directory of Social Change – provides training and publications on a wide range of issues including fundraising

0845 077 7707 www.dsc.org.uk

Locality (was BASSAC – British Association of Settlements & Social Action Centres and DTA – Development Trusts Association) – the UK national body for local community-based development, strong supporter of the ideas of community assets and social enterprise

0345 458 8336 www.locality.org.uk

NALC – National Association of Local Councils – offers a wide range of guidance including how to set up a new parish council in England

0207 637 1865 www.nalc.gov.uk

National Community Land Trust Network – provides funding, resources, training and advice for community land trusts and works with government, local authorities, lenders and funders to establish the best conditions for community land trusts to grow and flourish.

0203 096 7790 www.communitylandtrusts.org.uk

One Voice Wales – national body for community and town councils in Wales

01269 595400 www.onevoicewales.org.uk

Social Enterprise UK – national body for social enterprises

0203 589 4950 www.socialenterprise.org.uk

Transition Network – more of a national and international movement than an organisation, but the website has a host of links to useful information

www.transitionnetwork.org

There is also the website www.placemakingresource.com, supported by Haymarket 'the producers of Regeneration & Renewal, Planning and the sold out Placemaking Awards; PlacemakingResource is the website for professionals working to make places better'

Index